AIClub Introduction to Artificial Intelligence

To our daughters, Danika Gupta, Ishna Ravipati and Aarna Ravipati.
This book is for you and your generation.

Contents

Unit 2: Introduction to Machine Learning

Contents

Contents

Acknowledgment

This book is a result of our shared goal to help improve AI literacy in the world from a young age!
We used our years of work experience along with our shared knowledge to create this textbook. We hope it encourages children to experiment and witness the power of AI themselves. We would also like to thank all our colleagues who have helped us through this journey and over the years.

We would like to thank Nandula Gamage for designing and editing this textbook.

We would like to thank the AIClub team that helped structure the online exercises, python programming, and all the activity pages available for both students and teachers: Dr. Amit Gupta, Dr. Swami Sundararaman, David An, Shilpa Toro, Yamuna Dulanjani, Hasaka Malalasekara, Jewel Motiani, Naveen Atukorala, and Chathuki Navanjana.

We would like to thank Nandula Gamage, Firaz Nizar, and Chelsea De Lima for helping list, promote and distribute the textbooks globally. Special thanks to Dinusha Wegodapola, Shashini Tennakoon, and Vishwani Herath for handling all things from organization and planning to logistics.

We would also like to thank our families, especially Amit Gupta and Giridhar Ravipati, for supporting all that we do and helping us to create such an essential textbook in this new age.
We hope this book will help the next generation of students reach their truest potential and help increase AI literacy in the world!

Preface

Artificial Intelligence is a powerful technology that is changing every aspect of our lives. But it goes far beyond fun gadgetry. AI is changing the way companies use information about their customers, how privacy is managed, and how decisions that affect your life - from medical treatments to loan interest rates - are made. For our future well-being, it is imperative that this generation, and everyone after it, becomes "AI-Literate". This includes not just understanding how the technology works and how to apply it, but also appreciating its strengths and weaknesses, and as a human, forming opinions on how it should influence and integrate with our lives, our laws, and our societies.

AI Literacy is the ability to understand what Artificial Intelligence is, understand its role in our lives, and apply this knowledge to solve problems. Kids who learn AI are in a better position to pursue a variety of careers, not just in computer science. They are able to understand how AI will impact future jobs in all industries, and be able to apply their AI knowledge whether they become a computer scientist, a doctor, a lawyer, an artist, etc. This book follows the philosophy of 4Cs

AIClub Introduction to Artificial Intelligence

AI Literacy and the 4C's

The four Cs are Concepts, Context, Capability, and Creativity. We apply the 4 C's in all the material presented in this book. In each chapter, new AI Concepts are presented. Context for the concepts is provided by showing their connection with real life examples. In every chapter, a pathway to build AIs on your own is provided. This ensures that the student has the capability to build in addition to understanding the concepts behind it. Every chapter ends with suggestions for a custom project, where the student can create an innovation entirely of their choice to demonstrate what they have learned. This ensures that their creativity can be translated into real projects.

Concepts
Core concepts of AI. What is AI? How does it work? What are the different types? How can it be measured and improved? How does it use data?

Context
How are AIs used in real-life? How do AIs like Alexa, Self-Driving Cars, Recommendations, etc. work? How are they built?

Capability
How do you build your own AIs?

How should you interact with AIs in your life?

How can you create an AI to solve a problem?

Creativity
What can you do with AI? How can you bring creativity and imagination to life?

What cool new apps can you build?

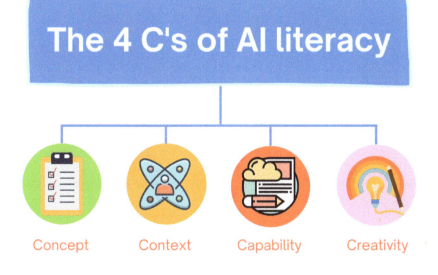

The 4 C's of AI literacy

Concept   Context   Capability   Creativity

Our vision is that the next generation of kids learn these critical technologies and in the near term use them to help their own future, both in college and beyond. In the longer term, we hope to play a role in empowering this generation to understand, manage and apply these skills and their own creativity to envision the future.

What is Artificial Intelligence (AI)?

Concept

Artificial Intelligence

Artificial Intelligence (AI) is a group of technologies that computers use to perform actions that come easily to the human brain. Human beings, unlike machines, have natural intelligence. Humans use this intelligence in their daily tasks without even thinking about it. With AI, computers can use smart algorithms to perform tasks like recognizing images, understanding text, etc. that would otherwise need human intelligence.

Artificial intelligence is a group of technologies that all have one thing in common. They enable computer programs to perform "intelligent" tasks that human brains can

Core concepts are added throughout the book to give you a better understanding of the terms used!

Unplugged Activities

Activity: Build a recommendation system!

Materials
Paper
Pencil

Steps: Answer the question below. Use the paper to make any notes you

Unplugged activities help students test their knowledge on the core concepts covered in the chapter!

Did you know?

Data Scientists spend most of their time working with the data, training and tuning AIs.

Context throughout the book will help readers understand the practical aspects of the terms used throughout including some fun insights!

AIClub Student Projects

Creativity

STEM AI Projects

Use AI to solve a STEM problem, usually by detecting/diagnosing a problem or forecasting the future. Run experiments to show how effective the solution is.
Examples - Find venomous spiders, predict the costs of medical insurance.

Creativity helps students use AI to bring their innovations, vision, and imagination to life through their own customized projects

Teachers Corner

Each chapter includes a Teacher's Corner containing additional information for teachers. The Teacher's Corners are divided into four sections: Core Concepts, Grade Level Alignment, Tips, and Curriculum. Core Concepts has an overview of the key concepts that students should take away from this chapter. Grade Level Alignment provides additional details on which concepts are best for which grade level (within Middle School and High School). Tips include additional ideas that we have found to work well in classrooms when teaching the chapter content. The curriculum includes links where teachers can get more resources for teaching the chapter.

Dr. Nisha Talagala is a world-renowned computer scientist and an expert in Artificial Intelligence and Machine Learning. The inspiration to write this book started with her experiences sharing the power of AI technology with her then 9-year-old daughter. She found that there were not many resources available for kids to learn and interact with AIs in a way that is engaging and not intimidating. She believed that, with the right tools and approach, kids can learn AI, become empowered, and create amazing innovations. She founded AIClub to bring AI Literacy to K-12 students and individuals worldwide. She is the CEO of AIClub and has many years of experience in introducing technologies like Artificial Intelligence to new learners from students to professionals. Previously, Dr. Talagala co-founded ParallelM which pioneered the MLOps practice of managing Machine Learning in production for enterprises - acquired by DataRobot. She is a recognized leader in the operational machine learning space, having also driven the USENIX Operational ML Conference, the first industry/academic conference on production AI/ML. Before this, she was a Fellow at SanDisk and Fellow/Lead Architect at Fusion-io, where she worked on innovation in non-volatile memory technologies and applications. Dr. Talagala has more than 20 years of expertise in enterprise software development, distributed systems, technical strategy, and product leadership. She has worked as a technology lead for server flash at Intel - where she led server platform non-volatile memory technology development, storage-memory convergence, and partnerships. Prior to Intel, she was the CTO of Gear6, where she designed and built clustered computing caches for high-performance I/O environments. Dr. Talagala earned her Ph.D. at UC Berkeley where she did research on clusters and distributed systems. She holds 73 patents in distributed systems and software, over 25 refereed research publications, is a frequent speaker at industry and academic events, and is a contributing writer to Forbes and other publications.

Dr. Sindhu Ghanta is an expert in Artificial Intelligence and Machine Learning, with several publications and talks in world-class journals and conferences. This book is an expression of her passion for teaching and making this amazing technology accessible to young minds. She is the co-founder of AIClub and works as the Head of Machine Learning. She received her Ph.D. degree in Electrical and Computer engineering from Northeastern University. After this, she worked as a Post-Doctoral Fellow with BIDMC in the Department of Pathology, Harvard Medical School, where she was involved in the detection and classification of features from histopathological (breast cancer) images. After this, she worked as a research scientist with Parallel Machines on monitoring the health of machine learning algorithms. She has done foundational work in ML health and operations in production and has many publications in the area.

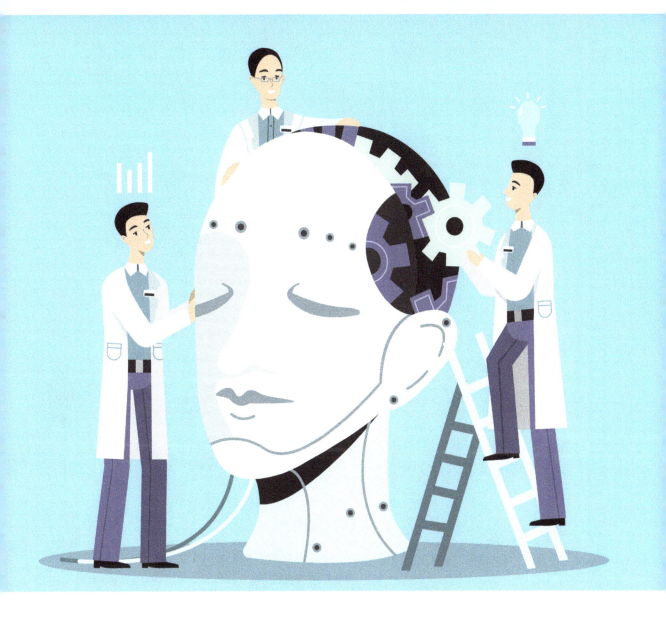

CHAPTER

1

Fundamentals of Artificial Intelligence

In this chapter, we cover the basics of Artificial Intelligence. We will go through the core concepts of AI and explore some practical uses for AIs that are around all of us!

What is Artificial Intelligence (AI)?

Concept

Artificial Intelligence

Artificial Intelligence (AI) is a group of technologies that computers use to perform actions that come easily to the human brain. Human beings, unlike machines, have natural intelligence. Humans use this intelligence in their daily tasks without even thinking about it. With AI, computers can use smart algorithms to perform tasks like recognizing images, understanding text, etc. which would otherwise need human intelligence.

Artificial intelligence is a group of technologies that all have one thing in common. They enable computer programs to perform *intelligent* tasks that human brains can naturally do. AI is not one technology - it is an umbrella term for a large collection of computer techniques. For example, a digital assistant in your home that recognizes your voice and responds to you is a type of AI. Another example of AI is recommendation systems, where websites like Netflix use AI to recommend what you might like to watch, based on what you have watched so far.

Figure 1.1 Devices with AI

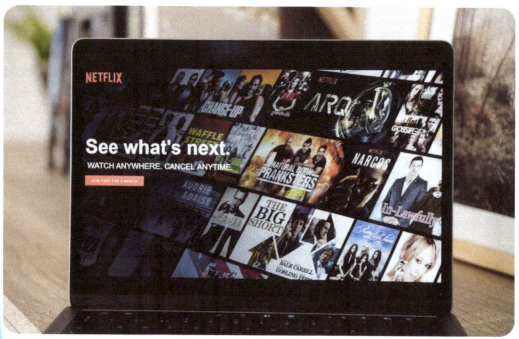

Figure 1.2 AI recommender

Humans display many natural types of intelligence. For example, humans can easily understand what someone is saying to them, even if the speaker is a little mumbled, has an accent, or has background noise around them. Finding the speech pattern and what the speaker is saying, even with distractions, is easy for humans. However, this is hard for computers. It requires a type of AI called Speech Recognition.

Figure 1.3 Humans performing normal tasks

Humans can make some estimates or guesses about the future (sometimes correctly!). We often try to predict what might happen in the future based on things that have happened in the past or things that we have heard about. AIs can also learn patterns from the past and use these patterns to forecast the future.

These are things that come very easily to the human brain, but can be extremely difficult for computer programs.

Humans can detect if something is unusual. For example, if we go to the kitchen and find it on fire, we know that this is not normal. We know this because we have learned what a normal kitchen should be like. Similarly, AIs can also learn what normal is and tell when something is not normal. This type of AI is called Anomaly Detection.

Finally, humans can see and recognize things around us simply by looking at them. AIs can also be taught to do this - it is called Object Recognition.

Humans are constantly trying to figure out how to automate things and decrease the amount of work we have to do. AIs play a big part in that. By teaching computers how to do some things that humans can do, we can automate many tasks and free up humans to work on harder problems that computers cannot handle.

Figure 1.4 AI being incorporated around the world

For example, in medicine, a machine can take an eye scan of a patient, but a medical expert is required to read the scan to tell whether the eye is healthy. In some countries, there aren't enough medical experts to read everyone's eye scans. An AI can be taught to read the scan and select which patients need to see a doctor. If an AI can automate this - it does not replace the doctor. It just means that the doctor can now treat many more patients because the AI can help the doctor understand which patients are most at risk.

Artificial Intelligence Around Us

There are many AI's that exist in our daily lives. For example, if you have ever gone to Netflix and watched a movie - you have likely interacted with an AI. After the movie, if Netflix has recommended other movies that you might like to watch, that is an example of artificial intelligence. This kind of AI is called product recommendations. It learns from user patterns and predicts what you might like based on what else you have watched and what other people like you have watched.

Figure 1.5 Netflix recommender

Product recommendations are on many websites today. For example, on websites like Amazon, if you decided to buy something, it will recommend other things for you to buy. It will also tell you about things that other people who bought the same product have been interested in.

Another cool application of AI is Digital assistants. You will find them on your smartphone, Google Home, Alexa, Siri, etc. They can answer questions, set alarms, play music, and so on. They use AIs because they need to understand your voice, understand what you are saying, and respond.

Figure 1.6 Amazon recommender

Figures 1.7 Digital assistants on phones and at home

Figure 1.8 AI's using facial recognition

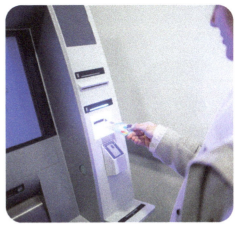

Figure 1.9 ATM's using AI

There are also many AIs in daily life that are not as visible. For example, AIs in banks help to detect credit card fraud. If you get a call from your credit card company and they are telling you that there is suspicious activity on your credit card, it is usually an AI that spotted that. Similarly, AIs are used to approve loans, detect diseases, forecast sales for a business, and more.

These are all different examples of AI in real life and they are all computer programs that are trying to do the kinds of things that humans can do. So, are all these different AIs or one big brain? One of the biggest differences between AIs and humans is that human intelligence is all in our one brain. AIs are specialized for specific tasks.

For example, the AI in your digital assistant is likely not able to detect credit card fraud. Similarly, an AI that approves loans is probably not programmed to play music for you or recommend movies. Each AI is taught to do a very specific job. Given that, some AIs can be very good at their job - and can even beat a human at it! However, humans are very good at generalized intelligence - learning how to do many things and combining what has been learned.

Figures 1.10 AIs in real life

Benefits of AI

AI is already being used in nearly every commercial industry. Every day, people discover new things that they can do with AI and new benefits that it can provide. This is one of the greatest strengths of an AI. When we can teach a computer to learn from data, we can apply it to any problem that we have data about. Below are some of the benefits that people, companies, and countries are seeing with AI.

1. Gathering Insights from Data

There are lots of hidden patterns in data that sometimes humans cannot see, because either the data is too large or because the humans are not looking for the pattern. AIs can be masters at finding such patterns. See some examples below.

Figures 1.11 Finding patterns in data

 Context — AI helps detect COVID

In 2020, researchers at the Mount Sinai Health System in New York found that people who get COVID-19 display a small change in their heart rhythms a week or two before developing symptoms. These small changes can be detected by their smartwatch. This means that AI can detect COVID-19 earlier than existing tests, and without any invasive testing or human contact with testers.

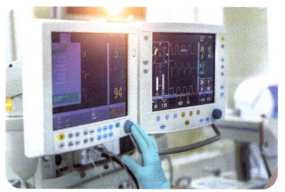

Figures 1.12 AI being used in medical devices

Fundamentals of Artificial Intelligence

Figure 1.13 AI detecting anomalies

2. Detecting Anomalies (Unusual Activity)

AIs are very good at determining what a normal pattern is and distinguishing normal and abnormal behavior. This can be useful in many real-world contexts to detect failures, fraud, etc.

Context

AI helps detect credit card fraud

Financial companies use AI every day to detect credit card fraud. AIs can study the patterns of each person's credit card use, and detect whether unusual purchases are being made. If this happens, the bank can call the customer and make sure the credit card has not been stolen.

Figure 1.14 AI detecting anomalies

3. Improving Productivity

One of the most powerful uses of AI is to help humans become more productive. We spend a lot of time every day doing simple things that do not require much brain power but take up our time.

Examples are finding directions, writing emails, etc. Auto-correct for emails, GPS driving directions, are all examples that can help us offload these tasks. This enables humans to get more done and focus our brains on more complex tasks.

Figure 1.15 AI improving productivity

AI in translation

If we recorded a video and want to translate it to a different language, AIs can do this automatically. This saves a human the time it takes to write down what the first video said, translate it, and then convert it back into voice in a second language.

4. Automation

AIs can also be used to automate tasks. Initially, simple tasks, such as filling out forms, can be automated. Have you noticed that, when you are checking out of a shopping site, your browser automatically offers to fill in your credit card information? This is an example of automation.

However, filling out forms automatically is a simple software task that does not need AI. An example of AI in automation is a factory setting where an AI detects faulty product from pictures of the product taken by a camera. The product predicted to be damaged is then removed instead of being shipped to customers.

Figure 1.16 AI assisting automation

AI in automation is also a cause for concern - many humans are worried that AI will take away their jobs, and there is a very real threat of massive workforce displacement due to automation. This is also why it is so important that as many people as possible become AI Literate, so that they can work in a world where simple tasks are handled by AIs and more complex tasks (like managing the AI!) are handled by a human.

Figure 1.17 AI automated production line

AI helps improve efficiency

When Amazon replaced many of the workers in its factories with robots, it also created a program to retrain these workers to manage the robots. This was beneficial in many respects - the robots handle the hard and sometimes dangerous work, and the humans focus on what the robots cannot do - things that require higher intelligence.

Figure 1.18 AI-powered robots carrying out shipping

Fundamentals of Artificial Intelligence

Challenges of AI

While AI has generated a lot of value and benefits around the world, as AI becomes more pervasive, it is also generating challenges. In this chapter, a short summary of AI challenges is covered. An in-depth coverage is provided in Chapter 4 of this book!

1. AI Bias

AIs learn from historical data and from humans, both of which can be biased. AIs are also very good at detecting patterns, so they can extract out biases that may not even be visible to humans.

AIs that pick up biases in these ways can then propagate the bias by making predictions that hurt minorities or other underrepresented groups. Detecting and countering AI Bias is a major challenge which any person working with AI should be aware of.

Figures 1.19 AI bias when picking candidates for a job.

 Context — Example of AI Bias

COMPAS (Correctional Offender Management Profiling for Alternative Sanctions) was a popular algorithm used to advise the penitentiary system whether an inmate up for parole was likely to re-offend. This algorithm was later discovered to be biased against African Americans, which means that African Americans were much more likely to be predicted as re-offenders than Americans of a different race with the exact same profile. The bias in the algorithm was discovered by a 2 year follow-up study.

Figure 1.20 AI bias in selection

REFERENCE SOURCE - https://www.kaggle.com/danofer/compass

2. AI and Privacy

Since AI can detect patterns such as faces, companies and governments can now use AI in ways that violate privacy. As we buy things, browse the internet, comment on social media, or even walk down the street, information is being gathered about us through our computer, street cameras, devices in our homes, and more.

This creates many privacy concerns since we don't know what companies or governments have access to this information and what they may choose to do with it. There are laws emerging in different countries and cities to regulate what information companies and governments can use.

Figure 1.21 AI using facial recognition to store personal data

Context

Example of AI and Privacy.

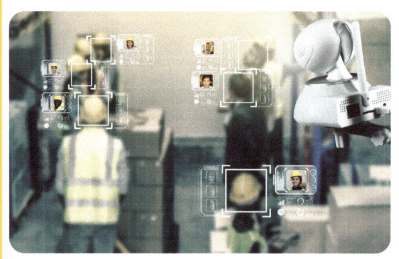

Figures 1.22 AI using facial recognition to monitor peoples movements

Cities in the United States San Francisco and Boston have banned the use of facial recognition in law enforcement. This is due to twin concerns about privacy violations and Bias.

3. AI and Equality

Countries all around the world are racing to adopt AI because they believe it will be an important part of their workforce being competitive in the global market of the future. There is a risk poorer countries will be even further behind because they lack the resources to learn AI, and even within rich countries, that poorer communities will be set even further back. Non-profit organizations are making free resources available to such at-risk communities to help them also learn AI.

 Context

Example of AI Bias - ImageNet Roulette

In 2019, AI researcher Kate Crawford and artist Trevor Paglen created ImageNet Roulette, a project designed to demonstrate how AI algorithms can learn Bias. They trained an AI on ImageNet, a very popular dataset that is used to train many image classification AIs. They then encouraged individuals to submit their photos to see what the AI thought the person's profession was. Many instances of bias were discovered, including African Americans being labeled as *wrongdoers* or *offenders*, and an Asian woman being classified as a *jihadist*.

This exhibition increased public awareness of the biases that AI can learn, and caused the team that created the ImageNet dataset to commit to removing over 600,000 images from the dataset.

Figures 1.23 Samples of images used to train the AI on ImageNet

REFERENCE SOURCE -https://news.artnet.com/art-world/imagenet-roulette-trevor-paglen-kate-crawford-1658305

REFERENCE SOURCE -https://www.theartnewspaper.com/2019/09/23/leading-online-database-to-remove-600000-images-after-art-project-reveals-its-racist-bias

4. AI and Environment

While AIs are capable of amazing things, building an AI (particularly a large and powerful one) uses a lot of computing power.

Figure 1.24 shows how much compute power it takes to train a large AI model once. Most large AI models also do not train just once. They train many many times.

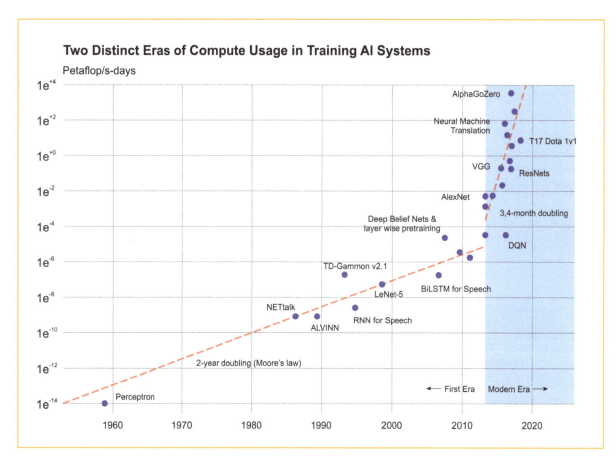

Figure 1.24 How much energy it takes to train a large AI model compared to other tasks

REFERENCE SOURCE - https://www.technologyreview.com/2019/11/11/132004/the-computing-power-needed-to-train-ai-is-now-rising-seven-times-faster-than-ever-before

Because of this concern of energy usage and carbon footprint, researchers are now looking to build efficient AIs that may not be as accurate, but are much more efficient in power and compute use.

Fundamentals of Artificial Intelligence

As AI expands, humans are finding that AI is both a benefit and a detriment to the environment. AI is already being used successfully in everything from wildfire detection to helping businesses streamline operations to be more energy efficient.

However, AI consumes a great deal of energy on its own, and generates a significant amount of carbon emissions. Researchers have shown that a single large AI can generate as much CO_2 as five cars in their lifetime. Because of this, new technologies are being developed to create energy efficient AIs that perform nearly as well as their energy-hungry counterparts but consume a lot less resources.

Figure 1.25 Responding to wildfires

Figure 1.26 Streamlining operations

History has shown us that technologies by themselves do not generate good or harm. Whatever good or harm a technology generates depends on how humans choose to use it. The nuclear technology that powers entire cities today has the same roots as the technology that caused Chernobyl, one of the world's worst nuclear disasters, as well as the nuclear bomb.

AI is a new technology with profound implications for humanity, and how it develops depends on how humans choose to shape it. AI Ethics is critical to ensuring that AI develops safely and supports the wellbeing of humans and the planet. AI Ethics is a multi-faceted topic (you will see more details in Chapter 4), and is still a nascent topic where new solutions are needed.

There are many other AI challenges that are faced by corporations that are building AI. They include how to make sure that the AI is not hacked (AI Security) and understanding if the AI can fail in practice, and how to detect and fix it (Production AI Health)

Figure 1.27 Shopping pre-COVID

Figure 1.28 Shopping during COVID

For sellers like Amazon, when the COVID-19 pandemic hit, buying behavior of people on Amazon underwent a drastic change. The top selling products on Amazon changed drastically from phone cases, phone chargers and legos to face masks, hand sanitizer, etc.

Behind the scenes, artificial intelligence (AI) algorithms are used for inventory management, fraud detection, marketing, etc. and such a drastic change in the purchasing behavior of people causes the algorithms to break. They stopped working as expected.

Figure 1.29 Fluctuations in demand and supply

For suppliers of products, an AI algorithm predicts demand based on historical information. The production system typically has flexibility to deal with smooth and periodic changes. However, a drastic change like the COVID-19 pandemic caused a sudden change in the type of orders that were being received. As a result, the algorithms used for forecasting and managing the production pipelines were no longer working as expected.

Fundamentals of Artificial Intelligence

1. List a few AIs that you interact with in your daily life.

2. Can an AI trained to do object detection, also recommend products? Explain why.

3. Fill in the blanks

(a) _____ is the term used to describe predictions made by an AI that favor a particular group of people unfairly.

(b) The type of AI that can detect different things in a digital picture is called a _____ AI.

(c) If an AI is particularly good at finding out when something unusual is happening, it is doing _____ Detection.

4. Name a few tasks that are very hard for the human brain, but can be done easily by the AI.

5. Explain how COVID-19 impacted the performance of AI for recommending products and why.

6. Explain with an example, how AI improved quality of life for humans. Pick an application of your choice.

7. Think about a problem in your community that you think can be solved by an AI. List the different types of AI that will need to be developed to accomplish it.

8. List some applications of AI in the medical domain. Explain the type of AIs that can be used to help in this domain.

9. Can AI completely replace doctors? Please explain.

10. Which of these things would be easy for an AI and which would be hard or impossible?
(a) learning patterns from data.
(b) predicting prices of houses if given past house price data.
(c) feeling an emotion like hungry.

Online Activities

1. Difference between AI and Robots

We will look at how an AI is different from robots and interact with a live AI component that mimics the type of capability an AI integrated into a robot's camera should have. Follow the QR code attached at the end or simply go to https://aiclub.world/activity-ai-and-robots to start this activity!

In this activity, we will learn
• How AI is different from Robots
• What Robots can do
• What AIs can do
• You can have AIs without Robots and Robots without AIs, but how combining AI and Robots can be really cool!

This activity has an interactive component where it will detect different objects that you put in front of the camera. Below is a screenshot showing an example.

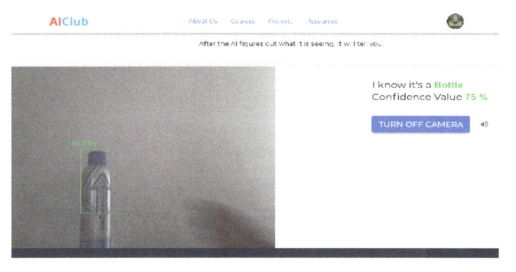

To do the interactive activity, you will need a computer with a chrome browser and a camera. You will need to have some objects ready, that you would like the AI to automatically recognize.

Unplugged Activities

1. Build a recommendation system

You will build a recommendation system based on a small set of data. Real-world AIs make recommendations similarly, but use very sophisticated algorithms and huge amounts of data with a lot of missing information.

Materials:
Paper
Pencil

Activity:
Study the table below carefully. It lists the customer's name and the first two books they bought.

Customer name	First book series bought	Second book series bought
Fred	Agatha Christie	Tom Clancy
Claire	Tom Clancy	Agatha Christie
Emma	Harry Potter	Percy Jackson
James	Harry Potter	Percy Jackson
Bob	Jane Austen	Emily Bronte

A new customer, Alice, has already bought the Harry Potter books. What book would you recommend? Why?

2. Group Discussion

Imagine a classroom where there are cameras around the room to continuously analyze the attention being paid by students in the class. Each day, the AI generates a report on each student, which is published in a portal that can be viewed only by the student, their teachers and parents.

Activity:
Discuss the pros and cons of this approach and the ethical aspects of monitoring behavior using AI.

Teachers Corner

Core concepts

After studying this chapter, students should be able to understand the following:

- What Artificial Intelligence is
- Types of AI
- How AI is used around the world and in their lives
- Some of the challenges that the world faces as AI grows

Grade level alignment

The contents of this chapter are accessible to students in any middle school or high school grade level. High School students are likely to appreciate the examples and challenges in more depth, particularly as they relate to AI Bias and other AI Challenges.

Some tips for teaching this chapter:

Most students have likely interacted with at least one AI in their lives (maybe even on the very same day that they study the topics!). Encourage discussions where the students explore AIs around them and whether the examples they bring up are AIs or not.

Encourage students to imagine what AI may be able to create in the future, or what they would like to see AI be able to do in the future. As they study more chapters, they will be able to see whether their ideas are already possible or whether they can become possible in the future.

Curriculum

Full curriculum covering chapters 1-10 is available at https://aiclub.world/teachers-material-book-volume-1
Curriculum for Unit 1 (Chapters 1-4) is available at https://aiclub.world/teachers-material-introduction-to-ai. Our teacher's curriculum include lesson guides, videos, presentation material, additional exercises, and assessments, as well as online support.

Teachers Corner

Scan the QR code for the Unit 1 curriculum (Chapters 1-4)

Scan the QR code for the teachers curriculum of this book

Assessment Key

Answer key to the assessment questions in the book can be found here: https://aiclub.world/teachers-material-introduction-to-ai

2

How AIs Learn

In this chapter, different types of AI are described along with how an AI learns, and all the different stages involved in its creation.

Why do AIs Need to Learn?

AIs need to learn. This is a fundamental aspect of AI, from which comes many of its strengths and also its challenges. The fact that AIs can learn implies that they can get better over time, and that more information can lead to smarter AIs. Over the past few years, there have been massive advances in both, the techniques of AI learning (also called training) and the types of things that AIs can learn.

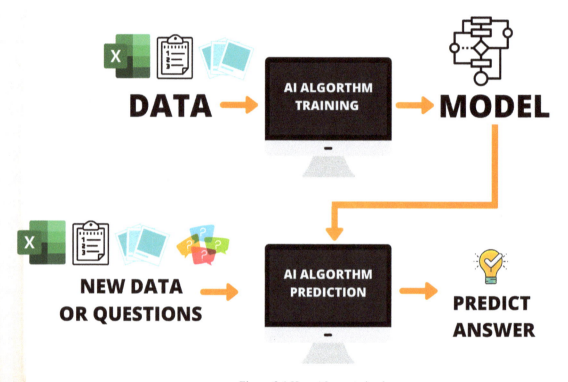

Figure 2.1 How AIs are trained

Once an AI has learned, it stores the information that it has learned in a structure called a Model. A model is the AI's brain. It is the repository of the essence of learning. The model is typically stored as a file, and depending on the type of AI, it can be as small as two values, or as large as trillions of values.

Figure 2.2 AI learning through data

Once an AI learns and generates a model, it is able to answer questions that it has not previously seen, based on the insights that it has learned during training. This phase is called Prediction or Inference.

Types of Learning

In this section, we review three of the most common variants of AI learning - Supervised Learning, Unsupervised Learning, and Reinforcement Learning.

Types of Learning

Supervised Learning

Lots of data that contains information about what needs to be predicted, so that the AI learns and can make predictions

Unsupervised Learning

Lots of data, but no examples of what needs to be predicted are given. By observing the data, the AI would identify patterns

Reinforcement Learning

Data is generated by a reward system that helps AI reinforce desirable behavior and learn

Figure 2.3 Learning through data

Figure 2.4 Learning through observing

Figure 2.5 Learning through a reward system

1. Supervised Learning

In supervised learning, the AI is given many examples of the types of questions it is expected to answer, and the correct answer for each question. By analyzing these, it attempts to discover the patterns that match questions to answers. The answer is called the Label. Since supervised learning requires the correct answer, it requires labeled training data, or data for which the right answer is known. In the example below, the data shows an AI whether a person is an Adult or a Child based on the *Number of Countries* the person has visited, the *Years in School*, and the *Height* in feet. The label is *Who am I?* - Adult or Child.

Concept
Label

The correct answer for a question, provided as a part of the data. An AI uses this information to train itself.

Samples

Each row is an example for the AI to Train with

Number of Countries	Years in School	Height	**Label** Who am I?
20	15	5.2	Adult
2	3	3.5	Child
10	12	4.9	Adult

Example of Supervised Learning

If a bank wants to build an AI to predict which customer is likely to leave the bank, it can use historical data about each past customer, with a label that states whether that customer left the bank. With such a dataset, the AI can learn the difference between customers who are likely to leave and customers who are likely to stay. Once the AI is trained, the resulting Model can be used to predict whether a new customer will leave or stay.

Figure 2.6 Bank statement of past transactions

How AIs learn

2. Unsupervised Learning

In this form of learning, the AI is not given the right answers but is expected to learn patterns within the data rather than match a data pattern to an answer. A good example of unsupervised learning is detecting anomalies or unusual behavior.

If a credit card is stolen, it is likely that the thief will use the credit card in a way unlike what the owner did. An AI that has historical information about the purchase patterns on this credit card can establish a baseline - what normal purchasing behavior for this customer looks like. Once the thief starts buying things with the credit card, the AI can detect these purchases as unusual and flag an alert.

Figure 2.7 Examples of unsupervised learning

Another popular class of algorithms in unsupervised learning is clustering. Given a dataset, clustering refers to dividing it into groups that are similar. One such metric of similarity is distance. Using this metric, the algorithm will cluster points that are close to each other. Figure 2.8 shows an example where the algorithms grouped the points into 3 clusters, where each cluster is represented by a different color.

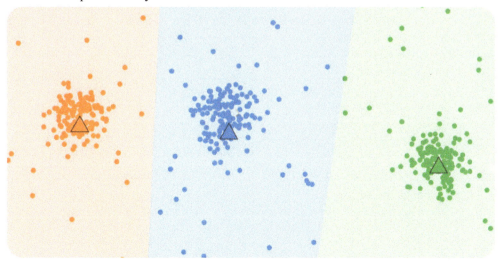

Figure 2.8 Example of cluster grouping

Context — Alpha GO

AlphaGo is an artificial intelligence (AI) agent that is specialized to play Go, a Chinese strategy board game, against human competitors. AlphaGo is a Google DeepMind project. The ability to create a learning algorithm that can beat a human player at strategic games is a measure of AI development. This AI has been extensively trained using both human and computer play.

Figure 2.9 The Chinese strategy board game Go

3. Reinforcement Learning

In Reinforcement Learning, the AI experiments and is given a reward for success. Over time, the AI remembers what experimental steps led to success and what did not, and becomes better at optimizing for the reward. Reinforcement learning AIs operate in two modes - Exploration and Exploitation. In Exploration, the AI tries new techniques to see what may result in a reward. In Exploitation, the AI uses techniques that were previously successful in order to get another reward.

Most AIs that play and win games are using some form of Reinforcement Learning. In this case, techniques are new strategies in the game, and the reward is winning the game. By playing a very large number of games over time, the AI can accumulate a series of winning strategies and become very good at the game.

Figures 2.10 Examples of reinforcement Learning

Data and AI

Many types of AIs learn from data. In the case of supervised learning, the data is the questions and the answers. In unsupervised learning, the data has no explicit questions or answers, but is presented to the AI for it to learn patterns within.

Real-world data comes in many forms and different types of AIs have been shown to excel at each of them. Figure 2.11 shows examples of different types of data.

Examples of data

Figures 2.11 Types of data

 Context — Where does all this data come from?

One of the reasons AI has become so popular in the last few years is that companies have gathered up a lot of data about consumers and can use it to create powerful AIs. Other types of data such as books have also become digitized. Rich data from video and audio recordings and data from Internet of Things (IoT) devices like sensors are generating large amounts of machine data. This data is now stored and ready to be analyzed, and AI is the key to learning the secrets hidden within the data.

Figure 2.12 Data from devices

Concepts

Sample	Each independent piece of information in a dataset is called a sample.
Features	Information that the algorithm is expected to use for making a prediction is called features.

Structured Data

Features			Label
Number of Countries Visited	Number of years in School	Height (feet)	Who am I?
20	15	5.2	Adult
2	3	3.5	Child
10	12	4.9	Adult

Samples

Each row is an example for the AI to Train with

Figure 2.13 Structured data example

This is data that is in some kind of tabular format. A simple example is shown in Figure 2.13. There are multiple columns, and in the case of labeled data, one of these columns is the label or correct answer. The other columns are a part of the question and are called Features. Examples of structured data include anything that can be placed in a database, like tables. These can be financial records, sales records, purchase histories, etc.

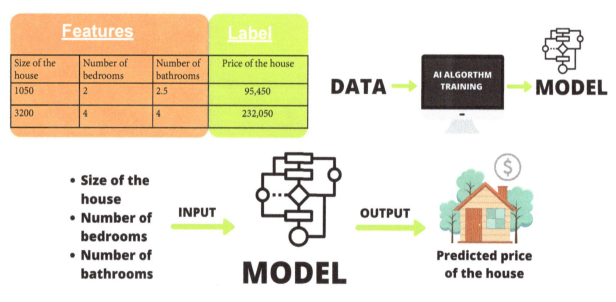

Features			Label
Size of the house	Number of bedrooms	Number of bathrooms	Price of the house
1050	2	2.5	95,450
3200	4	4	232,050

DATA → AI ALGORTHM TRAINING → MODEL

- Size of the house
- Number of bedrooms
- Number of bathrooms

INPUT → MODEL → OUTPUT → Predicted price of the house

Figure 2.14 Training an AI with structured data

How AIs learn

Figure 2.14 shows how structured data with labels can be used to train an AI. In this case, the AI is learning to predict the price of a house from the size of the house, the number of bedrooms, and the number of bathrooms. These three pieces of information are the features. The label is the price of the house. Once the AI learns, it creates a model which is then placed into a prediction program. The prediction program is given the details of a new house (size, number of bedrooms, and number of bathrooms) and expected to output the price of the house. The prediction program takes this information and processes it through the model to predict the price.

Unstructured Data

Unstructured Data is free form data. It can be text, books, music, video, etc.

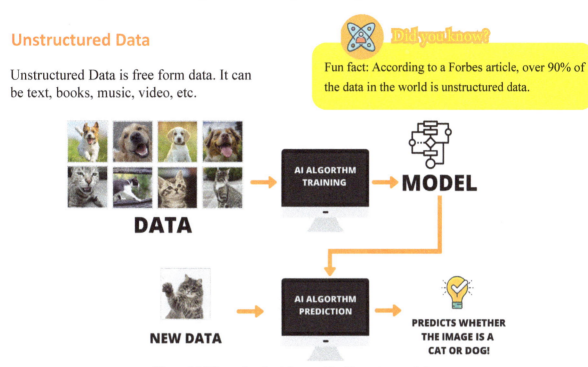

Figure 2.15 Example of training an AI with unstructured data

Figure 2.15 shows an example of unstructured data with labels. In this case, the AI is trained on images of cats and dogs. After training, the AI is given a new image and will predict whether it is a cat or a dog.

Context

How much data can one human generate?

In our daily life, every time we use an app, search engine, or even a device for that matter, we create data!
The amount of data we produce every day is truly mind-boggling. There are 2.5 quintillion bytes of data created each day at our current pace, but that pace is only accelerating with the growth of the Internet of Things (IoT).

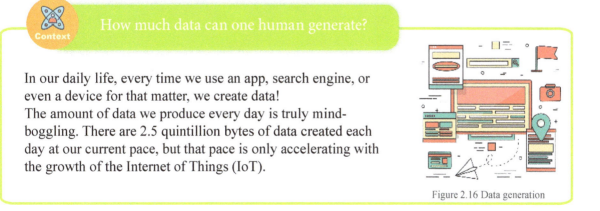

Figure 2.16 Data generation

Time Series Data

There are also other types of data, such as time series data. A good example of time series data is stock prices over time. Another good example of Time Series data is data emitted by sensors. For example, if you have a temperature sensor in your home that emits data every 5 minutes, that would be time series data. Since time series data is recorded over time, it is immutable.

Figure 2.17 Time Series Data

This means you can append to existing data, but not change the order of data that is already recorded. This is a special aspect of time series data. Other types of data, such as a collection of images or typical CSV (comma-separated values) files assume independence between different samples. This means the samples can be shuffled without impacting analysis or insights about the data. Each data point in time series is typically statistically dependent on the previous data point and that makes it a unique type of data.

Time	Temperature
5:00	37
9:30	38
1:40	35
3:00	40
4:30	40
5:00	41
5:45	38
7:00	38.3
8:30	40.5

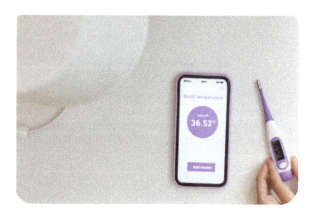

Figure 2.18 Monitoring temperature

Figure 2.18 shows an example of structured data without labels. In this case, the data shows the temperature of a patient over time. There is no label but the AI is expected to flag unusual behavior. If the patient's temperature rises sharply, the AI will detect it and flag an alert.

Exercise

How much data would it take to record a video of the entire human life?

Assume the human life span to be 70 years. One minute of data consumes approximately 60MB of space. Calculate the amount of data required based on these assumptions.

Figure 2.19 A human life in data

Stages of building an AI

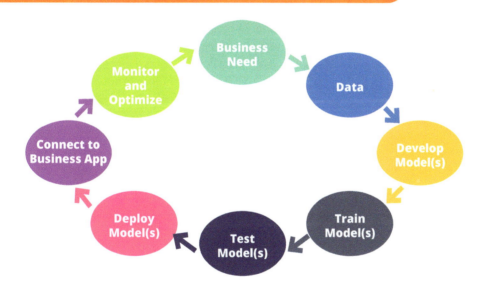

Figure 2.20 Stages of building an AI

Figure 2.20 shows a typical life cycle of creating an Artificial Intelligence service. While AI can be used to solve many types of problems, the steps of the life cycle stay largely the same.

The Problem

The first step is to decide what problem should be solved with AI. An example problem could be recommending new products to customers, or new movies or books. While defining the problem, it is important to understand what a successful AI would look like.

For example, an AI that recommends products would be successful if the customer actually clicks on the recommended products and ideally buys one. If the AI recommends products but you discover over time that no one buys the recommended product, the AI has not been successful.

Figure 2.21 A website recommending products

The Data

Figure 2.22 Amazon recommender

Once the problem to be solved is clear, the next step is the data. To recommend products, the AI needs to learn how things a customer has bought can be used to predict what else they may like. For example, if a customer bought balloons and cake decorations, they may be planning a party and might want other party supplies. To learn these patterns, the AI will need historical data about customers and their purchase histories.

Context Recommendation Systems in real life

OTT (Over-the-top media service) refers to media services that are offered directly to viewers over the Internet. Some examples of such platforms are Netflix, Disney+, Hulu, Amazon Prime Video, etc. These services typically have a subscription which users can sign up for and watch content. As a result, these services have data about what types of content different users watch.

Figure 2.23 Netflix Recommender

They leverage this data to train AIs that provide personalized recommendations to different users. The goal of this AI is to recommend a show or movie that has a high chance of viewership from you based on what you have watched so far. This AI uses information such as viewing history, genres, watch time, etc. about you and tries to match you with similar users and the types of content that they watched and you have not watched yet. The goal of these AIs is to make meaningful recommendations that bring joy to customers so that you continue to subscribe to their service.

How AIs learn

Training the AI

Once the data is collected, an AI needs to be trained. There are many types of AIs that can be used, so part of the job is to select a few types of AIs to try. Each AI is then trained to see how well it can predict future purchases. Each type of AI is called an AI Algorithm - a particular implementation of an AI. Most data scientists select several algorithms and train each and see how it does.

Figure 2.24 Training an AI

Figure 2.25 Training an AI

Context

How long does training take?

AI training times can vary substantially depending on the type of data used, the type of AI algorithm being trained, and the size of the data. Simple datasets, such as tables with a few hundred rows and tens of columns, can train in five to ten minutes for machine learning algorithms, with deep learning algorithms taking a bit longer. Images data, video data, and other complex datasets can take hours to days, or even weeks to train. Other advanced AIs, such as the AIs that create images or videos, can take even longer.

There are many hardware options now to speed up AIs. The most popular is GPU (Graphics Processing Units), created by companies like Nvidia. Other companies have also built hardware to make AI training faster, including Tensor Processing Units (TPUs) from Google, and special instructions in computers from companies like Intel.

Tuning the AI

An important part of training an AI is tuning it. Tuning requires measuring how well the AI is doing followed by steps to improve it. Each type of AI has a set of *Metrics* by which it can be measured (more on this in later chapters). While tuning, data can be changed, AI type can be changed, or each AI can be individually tuned to see how the metrics change. Most AIs have many tuning options (called *hyper-parameters* - you will learn more about this in later chapters). By changing the values of these hyper parameters, one can change how well the AI learns. In later chapters, different hyper-parameters of different algorithms are described along with metrics by which their performance can quantify the quality of an AI.

Concept

Training

Training is where an AI model is given a set of training data and asked to make decisions based on that information. The model will then use what the AI has learned to predict outcomes of future inputs.

Concept

Hyper Parameters

A hyper parameter is a parameter that is set before the learning process begins. These parameters are tunable and can directly affect how well a model trains.

Deploying the AI

After completing the previous step, the AI should be doing well on its metrics. Recall from previous sections that this AI has a model (a file that contains numbers describing what it has learned - its *brain*). For this AI to be useful, this model has to be put in a place where it can answer new questions. This is called *Deployment*. Once the AI is deployed, it can answer questions to solve the problem. For example, in the case of a product recommendation AI, deploying would mean running it in a computer program where information about new customers can come in and the AI can recommend future products.

Figures 2.26 Deploying different types of AI

Connecting the AI to an application

Once the AI is deployed, it needs to be connected to an application so that it can be used. For the production recommendation AI, this application may be a shopping website. Customers come to the website and buy products. When a customer browses a product, information about the customer and the product is sent to the deployed AI. The AI uses this information to recommend other products, and these recommendations are displayed for the customer on the website.

Figures 2.27 AI recommender system installed on Amazon's site

Concept

Deployment

Deployment is the method by which you integrate a machine learning model into an existing production environment to make practical business decisions based on data. It is one of the last stages in the machine learning life cycle and can be one of the most cumbersome.

Figure 2.28 AI being trained with images

Concept

Monitoring

Once an AI has been deployed into production, the process of ensuring that it makes predictions as expected under external variations in data, software and environment is called monitoring.

Monitoring the AI

Once the AI is connected to the application, one round of the life cycle is complete! However, it is very important to keep monitoring the AI to make sure that it is performing well. For example, AIs can break if the types of questions that are asked do not resemble anything they saw in training. AIs can also break if there are bugs (mistakes) in the software that built the AI. Some AIs are also susceptible to hackers who can try to break the AI. For all these reasons and more, it is very important to keep monitoring the AI.

It is very important that the AI is only asked questions that it is trained to answer. If questions that it does not know about are asked, it will not say "I don't know". It will give the wrong answer because it has no idea that it does not know.

And repeat!

It is very important to repeat this life cycle and continue to improve the AI. Sometimes this iteration happens because there is new data and a better model can be built using it. Sometimes while building the first iteration, ways to make it better are discovered. All real-world AIs iterate, and the more they iterate, the better the AI becomes at solving the problem.

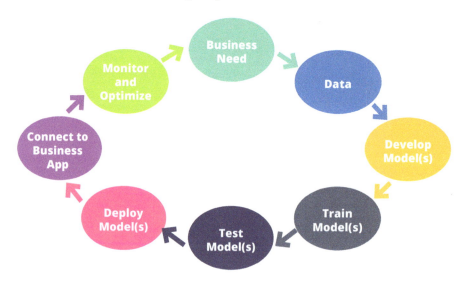

Figure 2.29 Stages of building an AI

Did you know some companies retrain their AIs every 15 minutes? Some retrain continuously! Others retrain only a few times a year

How AIs learn

When a movie star wears a dress

AIs learn from data, so the more recent the data, the more likely that the AI's knowledge is up to date. This is particularly important for AIs in environments where information changes quickly (like news sites or shopping sites). As an example - imagine that you are the owner of a clothing website. A famous movie star unexpectedly wore a dress that you carry. Suddenly orders for this dress skyrocket on your website. You would want to adapt to this quickly - and have your AI recommend this dress to anyone who may be interested. Adapting quickly is key, because this trend may not even last a few days - the moment some other movie star wears something else, this trend may end.

Figure 2.30 A celebrity wearing a yellow dress

AIs in the real-world can train as frequently as every 15 minutes, or as infrequently as once per year. The factors that drive retraining frequency include - how quickly does the data change? Does the AI need to pass any legal reviews (as they do in the medical and finance industries)? Will retraining the AI make it more accurate and bring the business more money?

Figure 2.31 Showcasing the yellow dress Online

Stages of Learning

In this section, parts of the life cycle where the AI learns are explored in more depth. In particular, how algorithms are selected, and how AIs are measured during training are explored.

Selecting an algorithm

There are many different types of algorithms available for any problem. Algorithm selection depends on the type of data and whether it has labels (right answers). Figure 2.32 shows a decision-making process that can be used. If there are labels, it is a supervised learning problem and one or more supervised learning algorithms should be selected.

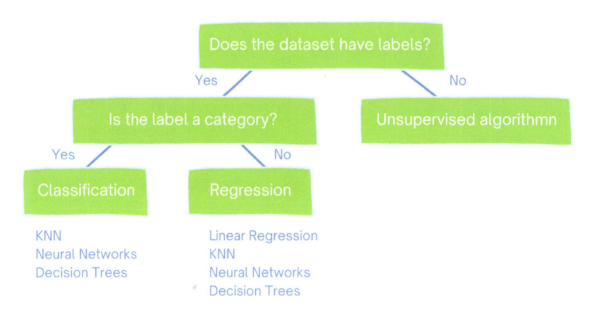

Figure 2.32 Decision-making process to select algorithms

If there are no labels and the problem requires the AI to take in data and provide an answer, it is likely an unsupervised learning problem. If the AI is expected to interact, make decisions and create strategies, it is likely a reinforcement learning problem.

Once the type of problem is determined, one or more algorithms can be selected. Later in this book, different types of algorithms and how to match them to data types are described.

Types of AI algorithms

Once the type of learning has been determined, there are several types of algorithms within each type. If a problem needs Supervised Learning, one can choose from a large variety of algorithms such as K-nearest neighbors, linear regression, decision trees, neural networks, etc. If a problem needs unsupervised learning, one can choose from a large variety of anomaly detection and clustering algorithms. Similarly, there are several different types of reinforcement learning that one can choose from. Given a dataset and problem type, the next logical question is how can one determine the best algorithm to use for it. This choice is made by studying the characteristics of data. In the case of supervised learning, if the label is a discrete or categorical value like adult or child, happy or sad, etc. there are certain types of algorithms that are suitable for it. Details of these algorithms are presented in Chapters 5 and 6. The distribution of data within the features can also give some insights into what type of algorithms will work well with it. Sometimes, it is not possible to estimate which algorithms will work well by analyzing the data. In such cases, it is common to launch many different algorithms and pick the one that is the best at making predictions.

Training and measuring the AI

Different types of AI are measured differently. In all cases, the goal is to determine whether the AI is behaving well and, once tuned, whether the AI is getting better.

However, the way the performance of an AI is measured is different for supervised learning, unsupervised learning, and reinforcement learning.

Figure 2.33 Training AIs using data sets

In supervised learning, since the dataset has the correct answer, it is possible to give the AI a test where the AI is asked some questions from the dataset and its answer is compared to the correct answer. To do this, the original data is split into two parts - the *Training Dataset* and the *Testing* or *Validation Dataset*. The AI only sees the *Training Dataset* while it is training. After the AI has trained and created a model, the model is given questions from the validation dataset and the AI's answers are compared with the correct answers. Common ways to split the dataset include giving 80% to the training dataset and 20% to the validation dataset, or giving 70% to the training dataset and 30% to the validation dataset. Some data scientists do select other splits if they feel it is better for their problem.

The amount of time taken to train an AI depends on the (a) size of data (b) type of algorithm and (c) configuration of the compute. Ranges of time taken to train an AI vary from fraction of a second to 6 months.

Context

Auto Machine Learning

Since there are hundreds or thousands of possible AI algorithms for any dataset, it is not practical for a data scientist to run them all. Enter AutoML. AutoML is a technique where a software program (itself a type of AI!) can take the dataset and run it against hundreds or thousands of AIs to see which one will train best on the dataset. Using metrics like accuracy, AutoML can then show the data scientist which algorithms perform better.

AutoML is now an established approach, with companies like Google and Amazon offering AutoML software. AutoML is part of a wave of Democratization of AI, which is to make AI accessible to everyone, not just people with Ph.Ds. Some argue that AutoML will replace data scientists, while others argue that it will free up data scientists to focus on other parts of their job, such as making sure they have the best data.

Assessment

1. How is time series data different from other types of data?

2. In supervised learning, what are the different components of the dataset?

3. Fill in the blanks

(a) _____ is the type of AI learning where AI learns patterns from questions and correct answers.

(b) The type of AI that learns by experimentation, and is great at playing games, is _____ Learning.

(c) An AI always needs _____ to learn and create a model.

4. What are the different stages of building an AI?

5. Given the below dataset, you would like an AI to predict the sentiment of a person.

Gender	Feeling	Mood
Male	jumping with joy	Happy
Female	headache	Sad
Female	holidays, yay!	Happy
Male	beautiful sunshine	Happy

What type of AI is suitable for it?

Assessment

6. List different types of data that an AI can learn from.

7. In an AI life cycle, which stages impact how performant an AI is?

8. Describe how an AI can be continuously improved after its deployment into production.

9. Once deployed, what information does an AI need in order to make predictions?

10. Given a fixed AI algorithm and training data, how can you control its performance?

Unplugged Activities

1. Build a customer feedback system

You are in charge of building an AI production system for a company. The company has several products as a part of its business. It gets reviews from customers who use each product and this is available in a CSV file. The business wants an AI to analyze these reviews and predict if a product has a positive sentiment or a negative sentiment.

Activity:
Write a report with details of each stage of the AI life cycle.

2. Think about the data
You want an AI to help your fellow students by predicting if they are eating healthy or not.

Activity:
Fill the table below with column names, that you believe are most informative for an AI to learn from. Once the AI learns from this table, its goal will be to take this information about any person and predict if they are eating healthy.

							Label

Teachers Corner

Core Concepts

After studying this chapter - students should be able to understand the following:

*   AIs need to learn
*   AIs learn in many different ways. Three common ways are Supervised, Unsupervised and Reinforcement.
*   All AIs learn from the information. Most of the time, this information is provided from data. Data itself comes in many forms.
*   AIs that are built in real life have a life cycle. The life cycle includes the stages that need to be followed to get a good working AI, and then the life cycle repeats to improve the AI.
*   Even within the life cycle, learning is a very important step that can have many stages.

Grade Level Alignment

The concepts in this chapter are accessible to any middle school or high school grade level. High school students may have had exposure to basic statistics and as such will be able to appreciate the link between data and statistics.

Some tips for discussions when teaching this chapter:

*   Encourage students to think about the sources of data around them. Do they generate data (for example from their internet searches, essays they write, etc.)? Do our shopping patterns and TV viewing patterns generate data?
*   How much data is out there? Encourage students to do a Google search to find out.
*   Is data growing? Encourage students to do a Google search to find out.
*   Without AI, what else can humans do with data?

Curriculum

Full curriculum covering chapters 1-10 is available at https://aiclub.world/teachers-material-book-volume-1
Curriculum for Unit 1 (Chapters 1-4) is available at https://aiclub.world/teachers-material-introduction-to-ai. Our teacher's curriculum include lesson guides, videos, presentation material, additional exercises, and assessments, as well as online support.

Teachers Corner

Scan the QR code for the Unit 1 curriculum (Chapters 1-4)

Scan the QR code for the teacher curriculum of this book

Assessment Key

Answer key to the assessment questions in the book can be found here:
https://aiclub.world/teachers-material-introduction-to-ai

CHAPTER

3

Data for AI

Humans are constantly learning from data. Data can be in many forms. Visual data such as the environment a human sees around using their eyes, audio data such as the language people speak, music, birds chirping, etc. Humans receive data through the senses of sight, hearing, smell, touch and taste. Human brains naturally combine these learnings and help make decisions.

How does AI use Data

As seen in previous chapters, AI uses data to learn patterns. Real-world AIs can use millions of examples every time they train. By extracting patterns from data, AIs create models, which are the equivalent of their brains. These models can then be used to interpret new data and answer new questions.

Does more data help? Usually it does, but not always. If the problem is complex, more data can help the AI learn the true patterns that exist in the real-life problem. If there is not enough data, the AI may not be able to extract the whole pattern. On the other hand, if there is too much useless or irrelevant data, it can confuse the AI and make it harder for the AI to learn a good model. This is where data scientists come in. A large part of their job is to select and organize the data so that an AI can be trained effectively on it.

Data in the AI Life Cycle

Figure 3.1 revisits the AI life cycle that was explained in Chapter 2. Data plays an important role in this life cycle.

1. During *Business Need*, the problem that the AI will solve has to be determined, and this in turn, will determine what data is needed for the AI to learn. For example, if the goal of the AI is to predict which customers will leave a bank, the data will need to include examples of past customers who have left the bank and past customers who have stayed.

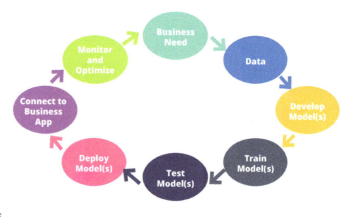

Figure 3.1 AI life cycle

By learning about both, the AI can extract the patterns that make the people who leave different from the people who stayed.

Context

Data for AI in Real Life: ETL

Real-life corporations process massive amounts of data every day for AI. This process is called ETL (Extract, Transform and Load). With ETL, companies get the data from its original source, process it, and store it for use by AI and other applications.

Figure 3.2 Extract, Transform and Load

2. During the *Data* step, all the data that the AI needs to learn from should be gathered. It should be ensured that the collected data is in a format that will make it easier for the AI to learn from. This chapter will cover the details of how this can be done.

3. Once the model is trained, it should be tested with data that it has never seen before, to make sure that the model has learned patterns well and not just memorized the training data. AIs that learned patterns well will do well on new data that has not been seen before (was not a part of the training data).

4. Finally, when the model is deployed and connected to the business application, it will continually see new data and will be able to answer questions and make decisions.

5. Over time, the model may be trained again. This can happen if new data becomes available, or better data becomes available. It can also happen if the engineers and data scientists find better ways of training on the existing data.

Context

What does a Data Scientist do?

Data scientist is one of the fastest-growing jobs in the world. As of year 2022, there is a worldwide shortage of data scientists that is blocking the growth of AI in the industry. A data scientist's job is to solve problems by finding the right data, preparing the data to be ready for an AI algorithm (called Data Cleaning, Data Preparation or Feature Engineering) and finding the right algorithms to train from the data and make predictions.

Figure 3.3 Data scientist working

Concept
AI
and
Data

AIs use data in many stages of the life cycle. Data is first used to train the AI, and then additional data is used to test the AI. Once the AI is deployed and in production, new data is presented to the AI all the time and the AI is expected to make good predictions on the new data. Over time, the AI may be retrained to accommodate new or better data.

Sources of Data

The AI needs data to learn. We can get data from sensors such as cameras, audio recordings, simple tables that record things like temperature, etc. There are many sensors in the world that capture data all the time. For example, surveillance cameras, phones, sensors attached to machines that record things like temperature, pressure, etc. All this data is saved as files in computers. However, unlike humans who are constantly learning from data, this data is not necessarily being used to learn and make intelligent decisions unless an AI is built.

The data that an AI learns from is typically saved into the hard disk or memory of a computer. A hard drive or hard disk drive (HDD) is typically found in all computers. A HDD retains the stored data even when the device is powered down. Whenever the device is powered up, the data can be accessed and is not deleted from memory.

There are several sources of data and we are going to look at some of the popular ones and how they are saved into the hard disk of a computer.

Figure 3.4 The inside of a hard drive

Camera

Figure 3.5 The evolution of cameras

There was a time in history when cameras were expensive and hard to come by for a large section of the population. With advances in technology, cameras are now cheap and easily accessible. They are on phones, security systems and everywhere around us. It has become very easy to use these cameras to take and share pictures and videos over the internet.

Cameras are a huge source of data and as high-resolution cameras become more common, the images and videos captured by them will be of better quality and will occupy much more space on the computer.

Phones

Phones collect a lot of data in a day. Phones typically have cameras and taking a picture using the camera collects data of a particular type called image. However, this is not the only data collected by a phone. A phone typically has sensors such as an accelerometer, and a gyroscope that collects information about motion. A phone can also capture audio data. For example, if you use the digital assistant service on your phone such as Siri or Google, it records your voice. The messages you type on the phone to communicate or post on social media are also data generated by the phone. In addition, apps installed on the phone can capture data about your interests and habits based on usage patterns.

Figure 3.6 Features on phones

Did you know?

We are generating more than 30 million MB of data every second on the internet around the world and this number will grow to be bigger and bigger over time.

Websites

When you log in to a computer and browse different websites, they can collect information about you and use it to recommend different products. Information about your browsing history is stored in something called a cookie. A website generates data about you which can be saved by different companies to understand your preferences and advertise products to you.

Context — How Much Data Can Sensors Generate?

Let's assume I wanted to record the temperature in my house. A typical temperature reading is 100 bytes of information (date, time, temperature, the ID of my house, etc.)
If I take a reading every 10 mins, how much data is that per day?
Answer: 6 readings an hour, 24 hours per day = 14400 bytes per day or 14.4KB per day
How many houses are in the United States of America?
Assume it is 100 million - that is 100,000,000 x 14.4 KB = 100 x 14.4 GB = 1.4TB of data per day from the US
What if we went across the world?
What if we gathered data for 10 years?

Sensors

With advances in technology, sensors that capture information such as temperature, pressure, vibration, etc. are available at a lower price, size and consume less power. As a result, there are sensors being used in devices all around us. For example, cars, washing machines, refrigerators, aircrafts, etc. have many different sensors embedded in them. These sensors record information about the environment around them at regular intervals of time. Some of the sensors record this information every second or even every millisecond.

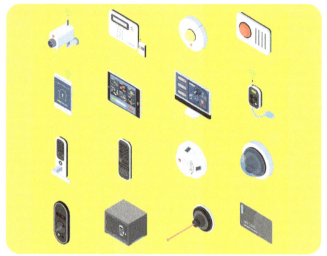

Figure 3.7 Devices that use sensors

Activity

Look around you, how many sensors can you spot?

Sensors are another very important source of data. They may or may not be connected over the internet. For example, older cars have many sensors in them that collect and save data about the car. However, they are not connected to the internet. For someone to access the data, they have to connect to the memory in the car using a physical cable. Irrespective of whether the sensors are connected via the internet or not, they are a very rich source of data and are everywhere around us.

Context — AI for Audio Data

AI can process audio data and recognize patterns in it to help the environment. For example, bird calls can be recorded as audio and AI can be used to recognize patterns in them that classify them into different types. This type of AI can be used for everything from nature education to tracking migratory bird patterns to studying climate change from changes in bird behavior.

Figure 3.8 Sound waves of a bird

SOURCE - https://aiclub.world/helping-nature-birds-machine-learning.

Types of Data

Data collected from different sources can be classified into different categories. This section focuses on four important types of data (a) Images/Video (b) Audio (c) Text and (d) Tabular data.

Images

Image and video data is typically collected from cameras, but is not limited to them. For example, medical images such as X-rays, etc. might be collected from a sensor that is very different from a camera. What qualifies as an image/video type of data? Image/Video type of data is typically associated with a width and a height. Within this width and height, image data captures information in the form of pixels. Pixels are a grid of data, where each point in the grid represents a single pixel. Images typically contain millions of pixels. However, one cannot see these pixels individually because they are very tiny and not distinguishable by the human eye.

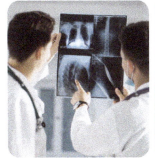

Figures 3.9 Examples of types of images

Context

AI for Images

AI can detect emotions from images of peoples faces.

Emotion AI, also called *Affective Computing*, is a rapidly growing branch of Artificial Intelligence (AI) that allows computers to analyze and understand human nonverbal signs such as facial expressions, body language, gestures, and voice tones to assess their emotional state. Hence, visual *Emotion AI* analyses face appearances in images and videos using computer vision technology to analyze an individual's emotional status.

SOURCE - https://www.technologyreview.

Figures 3.10 Facial recognition of emotions

Types of Data

Audio

Audio data is a digital representation of sound. This could be things like music, conversations, etc. which a human can understand, but is not limited to it. There is audio data that records the sound signal at a frequency that the human ear might not be able to hear. Sometimes, this audio data might sound like white noise to the human ear when played by a standard program on the computer.

Figure 3.11 Examples of audio in our lives

Figures 3.12 Examples of devices that give out audio

Context — How is data used in the real world?

Smartwatches and other wearable devices that continuously measure users heart rates, skin temperature and other physiological markers can help spot subtle heartbeat changes and provide early warnings about diseases like the onset of a COVID-19 infection.

Figures 3.13 Smart Watch

SOURCE - https://www.cbsnews.com/news/covid-symptoms-smart-watch/

Data for AI

Text

Text data is used to represent language. Different languages have different characters and symbols and together they represent language. However, text data is not limited to languages. Computer programs generate text data in the form of logs that record different information about the programs running. The book you are reading right now is also a form of text data.

Figure 3.14 Examples of text in programming

Tabular Data

Tabular forms of data consist of rows and columns. An example of tabular data is shown below. Column names represent different aspects of the data. Rows typically represent different examples. For example, in this case, each row represents a different person. Tabular data is used almost everywhere to organize data in a structured way. A very popular part of computer science called databases deals exclusively with the process of saving and retrieving such data efficiently.

CreditScore	Age	Tenure	Balance	NumOfProducts	HasCrCard	IsActiveMember	EstimatedSalary	Exited
619	42	2	0	1	1	1	101348.88	1
608	41	1	83807.86	1	0	1	112542.58	0
502	42	8	159660.8	3	1	0	113931.57	1
699	39	1	0	2	0	0	93826.63	0
850	43	2	125510.82	1	1	1	79084.1	0
645	44	8	113755.78	2	1	0	149756.71	1
822	50	7	0	2	1	1	10062.8	0
376	29	4	115046.74	4	1	0	119346.88	1
501	44	4	142051.07	2	0	1	74940.5	0
684	27	2	134603.88	1	1	1	71725.73	0
528	31	6	102016.72	2	0	0	80181.12	0
497	24	3	0	2	1	0	76390.01	0
476	34	10	0	2	1	0	26260.98	0
549	25	5	0	2	0	0	190857.79	0

Figure 3.15 Examples of text in tabular form

Files

A lot of data can be stored in files. A file is a collection of data that is in order (the first data is at the beginning of the file, then the middle, and so on). Files can be of varied lengths and can have human-readable names. Files are often named with extensions that describe what type of data it is. For example, a file *data.txt* would likely be text or numbers data. A file *data.CSV* would imply data that are in rows with every element separated by a comma. *data.JPEG* is likely an image in JPEG format. Extensions tell the computer which type of application created it. Typically, the same type of application can open the file we well. For example, the jpeg extension tells the computer that the data consists of an image and any type of application that can view images will be able to open it. Files can be organized into *Folders* which are also called *Directories*.

Figure 3.16 Collection of files

Databases

A database is an application that stores and retrieves data. It is particularly good to use databases if you want to select and query parts of the data. For example, if you own a bookstore and need to track every order, you can put the order data into a database. You can then query for orders on a given day, all orders by the same customer, etc.

Data that is in tabular format can frequently be stored in databases. Other types of data can be in databases as well. These days, a database can hold almost any type of data. It can also hold collections of files!

Figure 3.17 Processing in a database

Computer Memory

When a program processes the data, the data is usually in the memory of the computer that is running the program. Information that needs to be used immediately for the execution of a program is made available in the computer memory. However, the data may not be in the memory all the time. Most computer memories today are *volatile*, which means that the contents are lost if the computer is restarted. So your data will likely live in some other location, and be brought into memory when the program needs to access it.

Figure 3.18 Memory board

If your data is stored in files or databases (or in any other way), parts of these files and databases are brought into the computer memory when they are needed.

Storage

In the long term, your data will likely reside in *Storage*. *Storage*, unlike *Memory,* is often *Non-Volatile* or *Persistent*, meaning that if you turn off the computer, the data is still preserved. There are many types of non-volatile storage. The most popular today are *Magnetic Disk Drives* and *Solid State Drives*. If you own a laptop, chances are your laptop has one of these types of storage, and that is where your files and databases live. A cell phone also has storage, to keep photos, etc.

There is also storage you can access over the internet, like *Cloud Storage*. Cloud storage uses similar hardware, but is grouped and maintained in data centers (huge computer facilities). You can access this storage through the internet and keep files to access from anywhere.

Figure 3.19 Storage devices

Formats of Data

Data is saved in the computers in a standard format. A standard format is used so that different programs on your computer can read the data and present it in a human understandable way. For example, an audio file saved on the computer as a bunch of numbers needs to be played by the computer in a way that humans understand sound. Similarly, images, text, etc. should be presented on the computer screen in a way that human eyes can see it and their brain can understand it.

Images

Natural images are typically saved in formats such as PNG, JPEG, JPG, TIFF, etc. Videos are typically saved as MPEG, MP4, MOV, etc. These are the popular formats in which images and videos taken over phones and cameras are saved. However, there are several other types of images such as medical images that have a special format such as svg, nii, etc. Some of these images are in three dimensions and you need special programs to load and visualize them.

Audio

Audio files are saved in formats such as MP3, WAV, AU, etc. There are standard programs that can read the audio files in this format and play them as sound using hardware such as speakers.

Text

Text data is saved in formats such as doc, txt, rtf, log, etc. One of the most popular formats is the word document format. In general, all the messages typed on phones, emails, etc. are saved in one of these formats.

Tabular Data

Tabular data can also be saved in formats such as txt. However, tabular data typically follows the structure of rows and columns. A very popular format is comma-separated values (CSV). Every row is in a new line. Each item in the row is separated by a comma. An example is shown in Figure 3.15. This type of data is very popularly used for training an AI.

Data Type	Format
Images	PNG, JPEG, TIFF, JPG, SVG, NII, MPEG
Audio	MP3, WAV, AU
Text	doc, txt, rtf
Tabular Data	CSV

Figure 3.20 Data types and formats of storage on computers

Data Size	Context
Byte	A single character is 4 bytes
Kilobyte	1/2 page of email is 1 KB
Megabyte	A small image is 1 MB
Gigabyte	1 hour of video is about 1GB
Petabyte	11000 4k resolution movies would be 1PB of data
Exabyte	Several hundred Exabytes of data is transferred over the Internet every year

Name	Equal to	Size (In Bytes)
Bit	1 Bit	1/8
Nibble	4 Bits	1/2 (rare)
Byte	8 Bits	1
Kilobyte	1024 Bytes	1024
Megabyte	1, 024 Kilobytes	1, 048, 576
Gigabyte	1, 024 Megabytes	1, 073,741,824
Terrabyte	1, 024 Gigabytes	1, 099,511,627,776
Petabyte	1, 024 Terrabytes	1, 125,899,906,842,624
Exabyte	1, 024 Petabytes	1, 152,921,504,606,846,976
Zettabyte	1, 024 Exabytes	1, 180,591,620,717,411,303,424

Figures 3.21 The breakdown of data

Data Transformations

We as humans can process different types of data in their native form. For example, images, sound, text, etc. do not need to be converted into another form for us to understand it. AIs on the other hand only understand numbers. In order to enable an AI to learn patterns in data, the data itself needs to be converted into numbers because AI can only understand numbers.

Images

Images are composed of tiny little elements called pixels. You might have heard of the word pixels in the context of a camera. Cameras are described as having some fixed number of megapixels. For example, a camera might be 5 megapixels, which means its sensor can record 5 million pixels. A 10-megapixel (MP) camera is more powerful than a 3-megapixel camera because it is much more detailed.

If we zoom into an image to look at its pixels, they look like Figure 3.24. Note how each block is filled with a single color. It turns out that each color in the pixel is represented by a number. In the case of grayscale images, a single number identifies the gray color. For example, 0 represents black and 1 represents white. All numbers in between represent a level of gray color as shown in Figure 3.22.

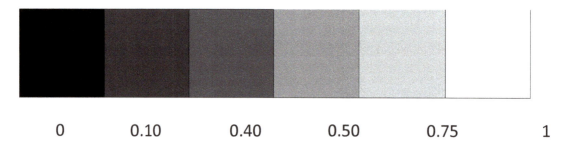

| 0 | 0.10 | 0.40 | 0.50 | 0.75 | 1 |

Figure 3.22 Grayness represented by numbers 0 to 1

Sometimes, the grayness levels are represented by numbers between 0 and 255 instead of 0 and 1. In a case where numbers are between 0 and 255, 0 represents black and 255 represents a white color. An example is shown in Figure 3.23.

Data for AI

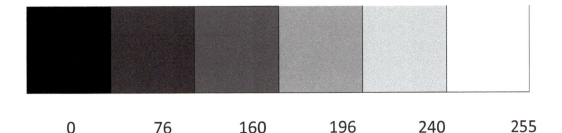

| 0 | 76 | 160 | 196 | 240 | 255 |

Figure 3.23 Grayness represented by numbers 0 to 255

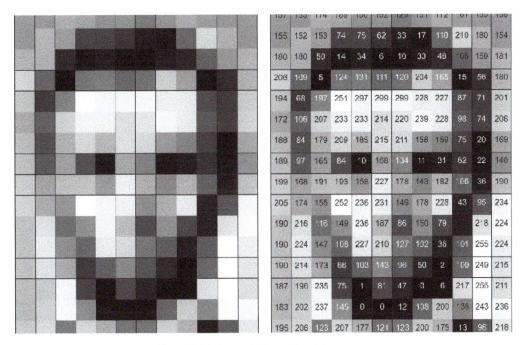

Figure 3.24 Grayscale image breakdown

In the case of color images, there are three numbers that represent the color (Red, Green and Blue). A combination of these 3 numbers generates the color seen in a picture. For example, if the pixel is represented by [255,0,0], it means the color of the pixel is pure red because green and blue channels are 0. Similarly, a combination of different numbers for the three colors represents different shades of all the colors seen on a screen.

This is comparable to the color combinations you see when mixing watercolors . A range of colors can be created by mixing the basic colors red, green, and blue. Figure 3.25 illustrates the different color scales used by computers.

An AI can only understand numbers and images are naturally represented by numbers assigned to each pixel and does not need transformation into numbers. Video data is an extension of the images data, where an image is recorded at different time intervals and when these images are shown on the screen one after that other at a rate of about 30 images per second, it forms a video with smooth motion

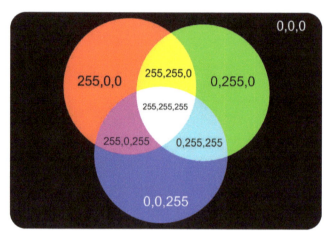

Figure 3.25 Color scale

Audio

An audio signal can be represented as a string of numbers. Unlike images, where one can see the entire image in one shot, an audio signal is played over a period of time. Therefore, it is a series of numbers, where the number represents the sound at an instant in time. A series of these numbers over a period of time constitutes the audio clip. For example, a heartbeat audio signal can look like Figure 3.26. Note that the x-axis represents time and the y-axis represents the amplitude.

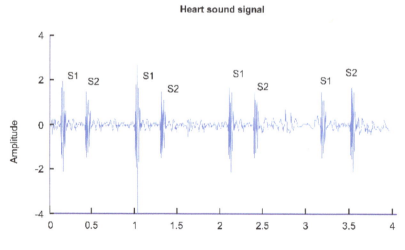

Figure 3.26 Plot of an audio signal

Data for AI

Audio data is also represented as numbers. However, its structure is quite different from that of images. The audio signal is a series of numbers over a period of time, while images are a series of numbers in two dimensions with no time associated with it. A video is a series of images, where just like audio, time is a factor.

Text

Text data is represented by letters and an AI cannot understand letters and words. This type of data is converted into numbers. There are many ways to convert this data into numbers. In this section, one of the simplest ways to convert this data into a table of numbers is demonstrated.

Take an example of two sentences in a dataset

| I love dogs |
| I love cats and dogs |

Figure 3.27 Sample text data

There are 5 unique words in the above example: (1) I (2) love (3) dogs (4) cats (5) and. These unique words are called the vocabulary of this dataset. Real-world datasets have 1000s of words in their vocabulary. Since Figure 3.27 has a tiny dataset with only 2 sentences, the vocabulary is also small.

Assign a value 1 if the word from the vocabulary is present and a 0 if the word is not present. A conversion of the two sentences into a table of numbers looks like Figure 3.28

I	love	dogs	cats	and
1	1	1	0	0
1	1	1	1	1

Figure 3.28 Converting sentences into numbers

An AI can understand data of the above form since it consists of only numbers. The above approach is popularly called the bag of words (BOW) approach.

Tables

Data in the form of tables can have numbers, sentences or categorical data in it. An example is shown in Figure 3.29.

ID No	First Name	Last Name	Grade
156753	John	Doe	5
145676	Maya	Deren	3
196764	Aisha	Sen	6
158766	Jane	Doe	4

Figure 3.29 Sample tabular data

Here, *First Name* and *Last Name* columns are not numerical. They are characters, but not full sentences. This type of data is called categorical data. Typically, you have a finite number of categories. If one of the columns contains text data, it would also need to be converted into numbers like the example shown in the previous section. Similarly, categorical data also needs to be converted into numbers. Again, there are several ways to do this depending on the type of categorical data. Categorical data can be of two types (a) Ordinal data (b) Nominal data. In the case of ordinal data, the categories have an inherent order. For example, if the categories are (i) very likely (ii) likely (iii) neural, there is an inherent order in these 3 categories. *likely* is closer to *very likely* than *neutral*. In such a case, simply encode the categories into numbers so that they follow this ordinal relationship. For example,

very likely -> 0
likely -> 1
neutral -> 2

The other type of data is the nominal data where there is no ordinal relationship. For example, the *First Name* column in the above table. If the categories were to be encoded as:

John -> 0

Maya -> 1

Aisha -> 2

Jane -> 3

Is it reasonable to consider that Jane is closer to Aisha than John?

The answer is, there is no such meaning or relationship between the numbers. However, the AI which consumes this data will imagine such a relationship. In order to avoid such misinterpretation of data, another method of encoding categories into numbers called One Hot Encoding is followed.

In one hot encoding, first step is to determine the unique categories in the data. Consider a single column *First Name* of the data shown in Figure 3.29. Each unique category becomes a new column with a binary encoding of 0 or 1 indicating whether this category is present or not. The table in Figure 2.30 below shows the encoding for a single column.

First Name
John
Maya
Aisha
Jane

John	Maya	Aisha	Jane
1	0	0	0
0	1	0	0
0	0	1	0
0	0	0	1

Figure 3.30 One hot encoding of a single column *First Name* from Figure 3.29

Remember that such encoding is needed for every categorical column in the data. Once all non-numerical data in the table is converted into numbers, it is ready for an AI to learn from it and make predictions.

Data Analysis

Data analysis is an important aspect of building an AI. It is important to understand the data that will be given to the AI for making predictions. Analyzing the data helps to understand which type of AI to choose for a problem. In this section, basic tools to help us understand a dataset are discussed.

Basic Statistics of Data

Statistics is a branch of mathematics that focuses on a scientific way of collecting, analyzing and summarizing data. It is a way to draw valid conclusions about data.

Figure 3.31 Visualizing data

Age	Grade
11	5
9	3
12	6
10	5

Figure 3.32 Sample numerical data

For the purpose of explaining the basic statistics of data, table in Figure 3.32 is used as an example. This table has two columns *Age* and *Grade*. This dataset is described using basic statistics.

The first term described is called *Sample Size*. The sample size is the number of examples in the data. For example, the sample size of *Age* in the above dataset is 4. This tells how much data is in the dataset. A larger dataset is considered better when training an AI.

Concept

Sample Size

Sample size refers to the number of examples in data. In the case of images, it refers to the number of images. In the case of tables, it refers to the number of rows in the data.

Another set of important things to note about a dataset is the minimum and the maximum values. For example, the minimum value (also popularly referred to as the min value) for *Age* is 9 in the table in Figure 3.32. The maximum value (also popularly referred to as the max value) for *Age* is 12.

Mean

Concept

Mean

Mean value, also popularly called the average value, is another important statistic that provides insights about the data.

Mean value is calculated by adding up all the values in the dataset and dividing it with the sample size. For example, adding all the values in the *Age* column results in $11+9+12+10 = 42$. Sample size is 4. The mean value is $42/4 = 10.5$. Mean value is popularly represented by the symbol μ.

Standard Deviation

Concept

Standard Deviation

Standard Deviation is a statistic that tells you how much your data deviates from the mean value

Standard deviation is a very popular statistic used to understand how spread out the data is with respect to the mean value. To calculate this statistic, two example datasets are used. They are also used to demonstrate how two datasets can have the same sample size, mean, max and min and yet have different standard deviation values.

First, standard deviation of the column *Age* in the table in Figure 3.32 is calculated. Mean value of this column has already been calculated and is equal to 10.5.

Step 1:
Calculate the difference between each sample and the mean value

Age	Age - μ
11	11-10.5 = 0.5
9	9-10.5 = -1.5
12	12-10.5 = 1.5
10	10-10.5 = -0.5

Step 2:
Calculate the square of the difference between each sample and the mean value

Age	(Age - µ)²
11	0.5 x 0.5 = 0.25
9	-1.5 x -1.5 = 2.25
12	1.5 x 1.5 = 2.25
10	-0.5x-0.5 = 0.25
10	-0.5 x -0.5 = 2.25

Step 3:
Calculate the mean of the value of the square of the difference between each sample and the mean value. This is 0.25 + 2.25 + 2.25 +0.25 = 5/4 = 1.25. Therefore, the standard deviation in the case of table in Figure 3.32 is 1.25.

Consider another table shown in Figure 3.33. Same steps are followed to calculate the standard deviation of this table as well. The goal of calculating the standard deviation of this table is to show how two sets of data with same sample size and mean can have different standard deviation values.

Mean value is calculated by adding up all the values in the dataset and dividing it with the sample size. Adding all the values in the *Age* column in Figure 3.33 results in 12+9+12+9 = 42. Sample size is 4. The mean value is 42/4 = 10.5.

Age
12
9
12
9

Figure 3.33 Sample numerical data

Step 1:
Calculate the difference between each sample and the mean value.

Age	Age - µ
12	12-10.5 = 1.5
9	9-10.5 = -1.5
12	12-10.5 = 1.5
9	9-10.5 = -1.5

Data for AI

Step 2:
Calculate the square of the difference between each sample and the mean value

Age	(Age - μ)²
11	1.5 x 1.5 = 2.25
9	-1.5 x -1.5 = 2.25
12	1.5 x 1.5 = 2.25
10	-1.5x-1.5 = 2.25
10	-0.5 x -0.5 = 2.25

Step 3:
Calculate the mean of the value of the square of the difference between each sample and the mean value. This can be calculated as 2.25 + 2.25 + 2.25 +2.25 = 10/4 = 2.25

The standard deviation in the second case is 2.25 which is higher than 1.25. This is because the deviation of data from the mean value is much higher in the second table than in the first one.

The spread of data across different numbers can be visualized using plots. This is a graphical way to visualize the data. Two types of plots (a) histograms and (b) bar plots are explored in this section.

Histograms

Histograms are used to visualize the spread of data between the minimum and maximum value. In Figure 3.32, column *Age* has the minimum and maximum values of 9 and 12.

Age	Grade
11	5
9	3
12	6
10	5

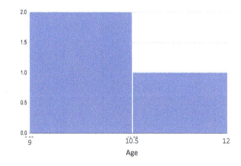

Figures 3.34 Histogram of data with 2 bins

A histogram is created that shows the spread of the data between 9 and 12. The first thing to pick when creating a histogram is how many bins it should have. For simplicity, assume the number of bins to be 2. This results in division of the range between 9 and 12 into two equal parts. The first bin is from 9 to (9+12)/2, which is 9-10.5 and the second bin is from 10.5-12. A histogram for this data with 2 bins would look like Figure 3.34.

For the same example, if the number of bins is 3, the data between 9 and 12 is divided into 3 equal parts (i)9-10 (ii)10-11 and (iii)11-12. A histogram for the data with 3 bins would look like the figure below.

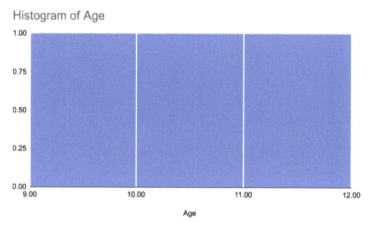

Figure 3.35 Histogram of data with 3 bins

In the real world, the datasets are much bigger and a histogram visualizes the spread of data. It shows how many samples are there in certain ranges of the data. This plot is used to understand if a certain range has more samples than the other.

Bar Plots

Bar plots are used when there are a finite number of categories. For example, in the table above, Grade can be assumed to be a categorical column with 3 unique values 3, 5 and 6. The number of times each category occurs is called frequency.
A table that counts the occurrence of each unique category is shown in Figure 3.36.

Age	Grade
11	5
9	3
12	6
10	5

Age	Frequency
3	1
5	2
6	1

Figure 3.36 Table showing frequency of each category

A bar plot for this table that records the frequency of each category is shown in Figure 3.37.

Figure 3.37 Bar Plots

Bar plots help understand how often each category occurs in the data. It is very useful to know this information. This information is used to make decisions on how to process the data so that an AI can learn from it properly.

Scatter Plots

Scatter plots are used to see how two columns of data relate to each other. In a scatter plot there are two axes: X and Y. One of the columns is chosen as X and the other is chosen as Y. Then a dot is placed for every data point to match the X value and the Y value. Visualizing the pattern of dots helps understand how the two columns relate to each other.

Age (years)	Test scores
16	164
11	118
11	116
15	158
9	92
11	113
15	151
18	186
11	120
17	180
9	91
18	182

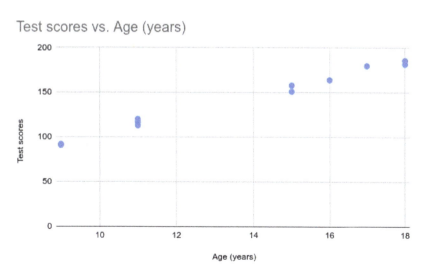

Figure 3.38 Scatter Plots

The above table shows a dataset that compares student test scores with their age. The scatter plot shows that test scores increase with age. This is an example of the type of insight that a scatter plot can provide.

Data Stories

It has been well established in this chapter that data is crucial to AI and it can come in many forms. Analyzing data is important to find out what is in the data and decide how to best prepare the data for training an AI. This section discusses an important related topic, *Data Stories*.

Every dataset tells a story. Why should this story be extracted and who is it for? Data Stories are frequently developed by data scientists, analysts or other engineers that work with the data. The purpose of a *Data Story* is to describe what the data is and what it tells us. Even before an AI can extract hidden insights from the data, humans can examine the data and find (possibly more obvious) insights using the analysis, statistics and approaches seen in the past few sections of this chapter. Further, the insights that the AI extracts can also be added to the story.

Good Storytelling - Know your Audience

Good storytelling has a few elements. The first - know who the audience is and what they care about. The point of a data story is to share with the audience, learnings from the data. What does the audience want to know? For example, if the audience is the CEO of the company, they may be more interested in high level items like how much money the company has made, rather than more deep details like how a particular feature of a product is doing. The person managing that product, however, may be far more interested in the second piece of information!

Figure 3.39

Concept

Data Stories

Data stories communicate important insights from the data to other people. Data stories help everyone who cares about the data to understand what the data is telling them.

Data for AI

Good Storytelling - Answer Questions

Sharing details may be fun, but ultimately, data stories need to answer questions in order to be useful. Think of what questions the data can answer, and then also what questions the audience would like to see answers to! For example, the CEO may want to know if the company made more money this year than last year, while a person who works on a product may want to know if the customers like the new version of the product more than the old one.

Figure 3.40

Of course, the data may not be able to answer all questions, but a key part of a good story is finding the questions that the audience cares about that the data can in fact answer.

Good Storytelling - Use Powerful Visuals

Data can be boring, but answers to questions are not. When telling a data story, visuals help the audience understand what the data is telling. In the previous sections of this chapter, different types of graphs and tables were covered. These can be used to decide the right type of visual for the data story. It is possible that the data story will have more than one type of visual.

Figure 3.41

Context

Why Data Stories Matter

When an AI is built inside a corporation, it is created to solve a problem. As such, many people in the company will care about how the AI is expected to solve the problem (these people are usually called *Stakeholders*). Many of these people will not be engineers or computer scientists. Data stories are essential to help them understand why the AI is expected to work, which in turn is essential to get their support.

Figure 3.42

Data Storytelling: USA Basketball

Context

In this exercise, a data story is explored. Figure 3.43 shows a public dataset about US basketball players (NBA Players).

Name	Team	Number	Position	Age	Height	Weight	College	Salary
Avery Bradley	Boston Celtics	0	PG	25	6-2	180	Texas	7730337
Jae Crowder	Boston Celtics	99	SF	25	6-6	235	Marquette	6796117
John Holland	Boston Celtics	30	SG	27	6-5	205	Boston University	
R.J. Hunter	Boston Celtics	28	SG	22	6-5	185	Georgia State	1148640
Jonas Jerebko	Boston Celtics	8	PF	29	6-10	231		5000000
Amir Johnson	Boston Celtics	90	PF	29	6-9	240		12000000
Jordan Mickey	Boston Celtics	55	PF	21	6-8	235	LSU	1170960
Kelly Olynyk	Boston Celtics	41	C	25	7-0	238	Gonzaga	2165160
Terry Rozier	Boston Celtics	12	PG	22	6-2	190	Louisville	1824360
Marcus Smart	Boston Celtics	36	PG	22	6-4	220	Oklahoma State	3431040
Jared Sullinger	Boston Celtics	7	C	24	6-9	260	Ohio State	2569260
Isaiah Thomas	Boston Celtics	4	PG	27	5-9	185	Washington	6912869
Evan Turner	Boston Celtics	11	SG	27	6-7	220	Ohio State	3425510
James Young	Boston Celtics	13	SG	20	6-6	215	Kentucky	1749840
Tyler Zeller	Boston Celtics	44	C	26	7-0	253	North Carolina	2616975
Bojan Bogdanov	Brooklyn Nets	44	SG	27	6-8	216		3425510

Figure 3.43 NBA players dataset

The first thing to notice is that the dataset tells details about different players, starting with their name and continuing with what team they play for, their jersey number, their position, their age, height, weight, and finally the college they graduated from and how much money they make.

Good Storytelling - Know your Audience

Since there is no particular audience in mind here, think about what questions one can answer from this data that would be interesting to people wanting to know more about the NBA and US Basketball.

Good Storytelling - What are the Questions?

What questions can be answered from this data? Here are a few examples
- Which teams pay more?
- How old are the players?
- Does age affect your salary?

These are not the only questions. Others can include whether height affects salary, whether some colleges send more players to the NBA than others, whether players from some colleges earn more in salary, whether weight matters, and so on. For this example, focus on the three questions listed above.

Data for AI

Good Storytelling - Use Powerful Visuals

The first visual shows the salaries paid by different teams, superimposed on a map of the United States. With this visual, one can see where each team is located as well as what teams pay their players the most.

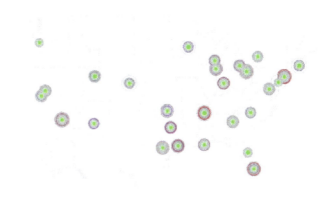

30,888   25,000,000

Figure 3.44 Plot of salary on geographical location

Age of Basketball Players NBA

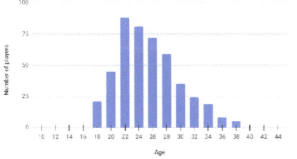

A histogram is used to showcase the age distribution of the players. Most of the players are on the younger end of the range, while a few players are notably older.

Figure 3.45 Histogram of *Age*

A scatter plot is used to examine the relationship between age and salary. Age is on the X axis and Salary is on the Y-axis. This scatter plot shows that the salary range varies widely for every age group, but most older players make less, while there is at least one notable exception.

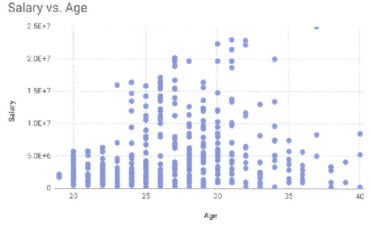

Figure 3.46 Scatter plot of *Salary* vs *Age*

Data Preparation (Feature Engineering)

As seen in previous sections in the chapter, data can come in many forms (text, images, etc.). However, all AI programs deal only with numbers. Before an AI can learn from the data, every data type must be converted to a number. This is one of many steps that are needed to *Prepare the Data* before an AI trains. This step is a very important part of real-world AI, and is called *Data Preparation*, *Feature Engineering*, or simply *Data Cleaning*. In this chapter, we will call it *Feature Engineering*.

Feature Engineering can involve many steps. Some steps are essential, in that the AI training will not work at all without them, and some steps are optimizations, in that the AI will work without these steps but will likely work better (for example with higher accuracy) if these steps are performed.

Reminder: Features and Labels

Quick reminder - data can have *Features* and *Labels*. Features are the information that the AI learns patterns about. In supervised learning (where the right answer is given) the answer is the *Label*. Unsupervised learning does not have labels.

Feature engineering has required steps for both *Features* and *Labels*.

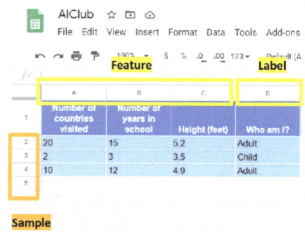

Figures 3.47 Features, Labels and Sample

Required Feature Engineering Steps

Some required feature engineering steps include
1. Converting every feature to numbers. There are specific ways that any data type can be converted to a number. We will not explore this much here, but you will learn about it if you study more AI.
2. Removing missing values. Real-world data can have missing values. These need to be either filled in or removed before the AI can learn.
3. Convert all labels to numbers

Feature Engineering Optimizations

There are many feature engineering optimizations that can help an AI perform better. Some examples are described in this section

1. Removing unnecessary features. If the data scientist knows that some features will not help the AI learn anything useful, removing them can help the AI focus, as well as take less time to train

2. Transforming features. For example, for many algorithms, normalizing a feature (dividing each value by a maximum so that the range is fixed) can help.

3. Creating new features (also called Feature Synthesis). For example, if the data already has distance and time, creating a new feature called Speed (Distance/Time) can help the AI if the pattern it needs to learn is dependent on speed.

Did you know?

That many data scientists spend more time preparing the data than actually training the AI? Feature engineering is one of the most complex and important steps in real-world AI.

Context

What is Dirty Data?

Real-world data is frequently considered *Dirty*. This is why feature engineering is often called *Data Cleaning*. Why is real data called *Dirty*? It is because data gathered from real sources can frequently have mistakes, missing values, or format errors. For example - if data is gathered from a sensor, there can be missing values if the sensor was turned off. If data is gathered from a video camera and the camera had dirt or water on the lens, the images can be of poor quality.

Concept

Feature Engineering

Feature engineering is conducted to give the AI algorithm a better shot at learning the patterns in data. Some feature engineering is required, others are optional but important for performance.

Example: Electric Vehicles

In this example, feature engineering on a real dataset is explored. This dataset is about electric vehicles. A sample of the dataset is shown in Figure 3.48.

ccelSec	TopSpeed_KmH	Range_Km	Efficiency_WhKm	FastCharge_KmH	PowerTrain	Seats	PriceEuro
4.6	233	450	161	940	AWD	5	5548
10	160	270	167	250	RWD	5	3000
4.7 N/A		400	181	620	AWD	5	5644
6.8	180	360	206	560	RWD	5	6804
9.5	145	170	168	190	RWD	4	3299
2.8	250	610	180	620	AWD	5	10500
9.6	150	190 N/A		220	FWD	5	3190
8.1	150	275	164	420	FWD	5	2968
5.6	225	310	153	650	RWD	5	4638
6.3	180	400	193	540	AWD	5	5500
5.1	180	370	216	440	AWD	5	6948

Figure 3.48 Dataset on electric vehicles

A quick examination of this dataset shows that it contains eight columns. Assume the AI needs to predict the price of the car (Column 8 - *PriceEuro*), then there are seven features and one label. Note that one of the features is a category (Column 6, which has two values AWD - All Wheel Drive or RWD - Front Wheel Drive). This column will need to be converted to numbers. Some entries in the columns are N/A (Not Available). These will need to be fixed. These two are required *Feature Engineering* steps.

Once *AWD* and *RWD* are converted to numbers, the new table looks like Figure 3.49. The *PowerTrain* column has been replaced with two columns - *PowerTrain-AWD* and *PowerTrain RWD*. If the original row had *AWD* - there would now be a 1 in *PowerTrain* AWD and 0 in *PowerTrain RWD*. This conversion is a process called *One Hot Encoding* which was covered earlier in this chapter.

AccelSec	TopSpeed_KmH	Range_Km	Efficiency_WhK	FastCharge_KmH	PowerTrain - AWD	PowerTrain - RWD	Seats	PriceEuro
4.6	233	450	161	940	1	0	5	55480
10	160	270	167	250	0	1	5	30000
4.7 N/A		400	181	620	1	0	5	56440
6.8	180	360	206	560	0	1	5	68040
9.5	145	170	168	190	0	1	4	32007
2.8	250	610	180	620	1	0	5	105000
9.6	150	190 N/A		220	0	0	5	31900
8.1	150	275	164	420	0	0	5	29682
5.6	225	310	153	650	0	1	5	46380
6.3	180	400	193	540	1	0	5	55000
5.1	180	370	216	440	1	0	5	69484
7.9	144	220	184	230	0	0	5	29234
7.0	167	400	180	380	0	0	5	40765
4	200	450	178	650	0	1	5	65000
9.7	195	250	153	210	0	0	5	34459
7.9	180	440	175	590	0	1	4	40936

Figure 3.49 Dataset on electric vehicles with *PowerTrain* converted to numbers

Next step is to remove the *N/A*s. There are many ways to do this. One simple way is to just remove the rows that contain *N/A* in any column. The other way is to fill in the *N/A* with some value - like the average value for the column, or the most common value for the column. All these options are ok - usually, data scientists experiment with them to decide on the best one. In his example, rows are simply removed.

Example: Electric Vehicles

AccelSec	TopSpeed KmH	Range Km	Efficiency WhKm	FastCharge KmH	PowerTrain - AWD	PowerTrain - RWD	Seats	PriceEuro
4.8	233	450	161	940	1	0	5	55480
10	160	270	167	250	0	1	5	30000
6.8	180	360	208	590	0	1	5	68040
9.5	145	170	168	190	0	1	4	32997
2.8	250	610	180	620	1	0	5	105000
8.1	160	275	164	420	0	0	5	29682
5.8	225	310	153	880	0	1	5	46380
6.0	180	400	190	540	1	0	5	55000
5.1	180	370	218	440	1	0	5	69484
7.0	144	220	164	230	0	0	5	29234
7.9	167	400	160	390	0	0	5	40740
4	200	450	170	850	0	1	5	65000
9.7	165	250	153	210	0	0	5	34459
7.0	160	440	175	500	0	1	4	40036

Figure 3.50 Dataset after removal of N/As

With these steps, the above dataset is ready for an AI to train (all required steps are done). However, it is possible to do more. For example, the columns that have acceleration time (*AccelSec*) and seats (*Seats*) have much smaller values than the other columns. One option is to normalize all the columns so that all numbers have values between 0 and 1. If this is done, the dataset will look like the below.

ccelSec	TopSpeed_KmH	Range_Km	Efficiency_WhKm	FastCharge_KmH	PowerTrain - AWD	PowerTrain - RWD	Seats	PriceEuro
0.2053571429	0.5682926829	0.4639175258	0.5897435897		1	0	0.7142857143	5548
0.4464285714	0.3902439024	0.2783505155	0.6117216117	0.2659574468	0	1	0.7142857143	3000
0.3035714286	0.4390243902	0.3711340206	0.7545787546	0.5957446809	0	1	0.7142857143	6804
0.4241071429	0.3536585366	0.175257732	0.6153846154	0.2021276596	0	1	0.5714285714	3299
0.125	0.6097560976	0.6288659794	0.6593406593	0.6595744681	1	0	0.7142857143	10500
0.3616071429	0.3658536585	0.2835051546	0.6007326007	0.4468085106	0	0	0.7142857143	2968
0.25	0.5487804878	0.3195876289	0.5604395604	0.6914893617	0	1	0.7142857143	4638
0.28125	0.4390243902	0.412371134	0.706959707	0.5744680851	1	0	0.7142857143	5500
0.2276785714	0.4390243902	0.381443299	0.7912087912	0.4680851064	1	0	0.7142857143	6948
0.3526785714	0.35121951220	0.2268041237	0.6007326007	0.2446808511	0	0	0.7142857143	2923
0.3526785714	0.4073170732	0.412371134	0.5860805861	0.4042553191	0	0	0.7142857143	4079

Figure 3.50 Dataset after normalization

So, did the optional normalization step help? It depends on what AI algorithm is used. Later in this book, two algorithms, Linear Regression and K Nearest Neighbors are described. Both can be used for this problem. The table below shows how well the first dataset (without normalization) and the second dataset (with normalization), did for both algorithms.

AI Algorithm	Normalization?	Error
Linear Regression	No	20047.2229
Linear Regression	Yes	18745.6863
K Nearest Neighbors	No	28241.3122
K Nearest Neighbors	Yes	12100.3289

Figure 3.51 KNN and linear regression errors with different feature engineering techniques

The goal is to get the lowest error (note that the concept of error is explained in later chapters). For now, the only things to notice are:
- Both algorithms benefited from Normalization
- K Nearest Neighbors benefited more
- Without Normalization, Linear Regression did better, but with Normalization, K Nearest Neighbors did better. So, *feature engineering* can actually change which AI does better!

Putting it all Together

What have we learned in this chapter?

We have learned that data is crucial to AI, and that data can come in many forms.

We have also learned that AI's ability to make sense of data is one of the reasons why it has become so valuable to so many industries in the world.

Data scientists play a crucial role in helping us (and the AIs!) make sense of data. Their job involves many aspects of data, from gathering the initial data, to doing Data Analysis and building Data Stories, to deciding what feature engineering to perform. All of these can make the difference between whether AI works well or not.

Where can I get data?

Where can I get data for my AI projects?
The good news is that there are a lot of public datasets available now. You can use these to study AI and even build your own highly sophisticated projects.

Some examples of where to get data
- AIClub Projects and Datasets: Over 500 projects and datasets for K-12 students
- Kaggle: A large repository of datasets used by students and professionals

Figure 3.52 AIClub website

Assessment

1. List different types of data generated by sensors around us.

2. What are the different sources around us that generate text data?

3. Explain the difference between a gray-scale image and a color image data in how it is stored in a computer.

4. List the statistics used for analyzing a numerical dataset.

5. Calculate the mean value of the following dataset with a single column of data [4.5, 6, 9, 2.3, 10, 15, 4.8, 12.1, 5.1, 2.8]

6. Fill in the blanks

(a) AIs need all data to be converted into _____ in order to learn from it.

(b) Converting text data into numbers by assigning a 0 or 1 to each unique word to mark its presence or absence is called the _____ method.

(c) Images are composed of tiny little elements called _____.

(d) _____ engineering is performed on a dataset to give the AI algorithm a better shot at learning the patterns in data.

(e) _____ are used to visualize the spread of numerical data between its minimum and maximum value.

7. List the different sensors that you might use in daily life. Which of these sensors is responsible for creating the largest amount of data in terms of the storage needed to save it?

8. What types of data does a smartphone collect? What are the privacy concerns with data collection on phones?

9. List a few optional feature engineering techniques. How are they useful?

10. What is the purpose of a data story and what tools will you need to create a good story?

11. What are the feature engineering steps that you would need to execute before the data can be sent to an AI for training?

Gender	Feeling	Mood
Male	jumping with joy	Happy
Female	headache	Sad
Female	holidays, yay!	Happy
Male	beautiful sunshine	Happy

12. What does the standard deviation metric tell you about a dataset?

13. What is a sample size, given a table with 1000 rows and 50 columns of data?

14. How does data analysis help with the process of creating an AI?

15. What type of plot would be suitable to visualize the two columns in the below data?

Gender	Age
Male	56
Female	23
Female	14
Male	27
Male	40

Please create the plots

Unplugged Activities

1. How much data is enough data?

AIs need data to learn from. But how much is enough depends on strategies employed by different algorithms.

Activity:

Using table 1, as a human, guess the pattern in data. Setup a timer for 2 minutes. If you are unable to guess the pattern, use the second table that contains more data with a timer of 4 minutes this time. If you are unable to guess the pattern, use the third table with a timer of 8 minutes.

A	B	C	Label
231.4	143.8	341.5	238.9
243.5	427.3	926.1	532.3

A	B	C	Label
231.4	143.8	341.5	238.9
243.5	427.3	926.1	532.3
23.3	41.2	67.8	44.1
3.4	5.6	7.8	5.6

A	B	C	Label
231.4	143.8	341.5	238.9
243.5	427.3	926.1	532.3
23.3	41.2	67.8	44.1
3.4	5.6	7.8	5.6
1.1	2.2	1.1	1.467
2.3	0	2.3	1.53

Python Exercises

Python code is provided in this module to help students get hands-on experience interacting with concepts covered in the chapter. The code snippets are kept simple and self-contained. All the code included in this book is available in a GitHub repository https://github.com/pyxeda/MiddleSchoolCurriculum/tree/master/Volume1.

A link containing the individual code snippets that can be opened in Google Colaboratory are also provided with each piece of code. When you go to the python notebook links provided with each code snippet, you should see an option to open in Colaboratory like the screenshot below.

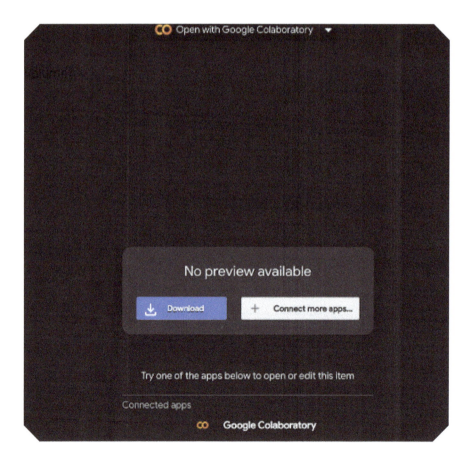

If you do not see this option, you might need to install the Google Colaboratory plugin in your browser.

Python Exercises

1. Read Tabular Data

What it does
- Reads a CSV file from Google Drive, and then displays,

1. A sample from the data.

2. Data from a selected data column.

Link to the code in a python notebook: https://bit.ly/3sXTY6z

Note that the above code can be opened in GoogleColaboratory. To view python code in this notebook, you will need the Google Colaboratory plugin installed in the browser.

CODE

```
[ ]  # Import pandas module to read the CSV file
     import pandas as pd

     # Import gdown module to download files from google drive
     import gdown

[ ]  # Please change the url as needed (make sure you have the access to the file)
     url = "https://drive.google.com/file/d/1J5z8OsAtgSp9i1eLxQFoxVexSZJuhI_-/view?usp=sharing"

     # Derive the file id from the url
     file_id = url.split('/')[-2]

     # Derive the download url of the file
     download_url = 'https://drive.google.com/uc?id=' + file_id

     # Give the file name you want to save it
     file_name = "child_vs_adult.csv"

     # Derive the file location
     file_location = "/content/" + file_name
```

Python Exercises

```
[ ]  # Download the file from drive
     gdown.download(download_url, file_location, quiet=False)

     # Read the CSV file
     data = pd.read_csv(file_location)

     Downloading...
     From: https://drive.google.com/uc?id=1J5z8OsAtgSp9i1eLxQFoxVexSZJuhI_-
     To: /content/child_vs_adult.csv
     100%|████████| 76.4k/76.4k [00:00<00:00, 2.44MB/s]

[ ]  # Print a sample (first row) from the tabular data
     print('---------- A Sample (first row) from the Dataset ----------')
     print(data.head(1))

     ---------- A Sample (first row) from the Dataset ----------
        num_countries  years_school  height who_am_I
     0              0             4    4.86    child

[ ]  # See the column names in the table
     column_names = data.columns
     print('---------- Column Names in the Table ----------')
     for column in column_names:
         print (column)

     ---------- Column Names in the Table ----------
     num_countries
     years_school
     height
     who_am_I

[ ]  # You can change the column name as you needed, after visualizing the column names at the above step
     column_name = "height"

     # Print specific column data from the tabular data
     print('---------- Data from the Column ----------')
     column = data[[column_name]]
     print (column)

     ---------- Data from the Column ----------
           height
     0       4.86
     1       5.79
     2       5.63
     3       4.86
     4       6.00
     ...      ...
     4995    5.33
     4996    2.83
     4997    5.61
     4998    5.32
     4999    5.21

     [5000 rows x 1 columns]
```

Python Exercises

2. Read Text Data

What it does
 - Read text data in python and print line by line.

Link to the code in a python notebook: https://bit.ly/3IbWTPg

Note that the above code can be opened in GoogleColaboratory. To view python code in this notebook, you will need the Google Colaboratory plugin installed in the browser.

CODE

```
[ ]  # Import gdown module to download files from google drive
     import gdown


[ ]  # Please change the URL as needed

     url = 'https://drive.google.com/file/d/1ydfmj1HosSIUtT7LnJL05cfLsItgMqqo/view?usp=sharing'

     # Derive the file id from the URL
     file_id = url.split('/')[-2]

     # Derive the download url of the the file
     download_url = 'https://drive.google.com/uc?id=' + file_id

     # Give the location you want to save it in your local machine
     file_location = r'about_us.txt'

[ ]  # Download the file from drive to your local machine
     gdown.download(download_url, file_location, quiet=False)

     # Open the file in the specified location
     with open(file_location, 'r') as file:

       # Read the file
       lines = file.readlines()
```

Python Exercises

```python
# Initialize line count
line_count = 0

# Print each line of the text
for line in lines:
    line_count += 1
    print(f'line {line_count}: {line}')
```

Python Exercises

3. Read Audio Data

What it does
- This Python program reads an audio file in the provided file location, and plays it.

Link to the code in a python notebook: https://bit.ly/3JOseIt

Note that the above code can be opened in GoogleColaboratory. To view python code in this notebook, you will need the Google Colaboratory plugin installed in the browser.

CODE

```
[ ]  # Import IPython module to play the audio in the notebook
     import IPython

     # Import gdown module to download files from google drive
     import gdown


[ ]  # Please change the URL as needed (make sure you have the access to the file)

     url = 'https://drive.google.com/file/d/1K7izykrla-qEuekekLayfGddml17calY/view?usp=sharing'

     # Derive the file id from the URL
     file_id = url.split('/')[-2]

     # Derive the download url of the file
     download_url = 'https://drive.google.com/uc?id=' + file_id

     # Give the location you want to save it in your local machine
     file_location = r'children_1.mp3'

[ ]  # Download the file from drive to your local machine
     gdown.download(download_url, file_location, quiet=False)

     # Play the downloaded audio file
     IPython.display.Audio(file_location, autoplay=True)
```

Python Exercises

4. Read Image Data

What it does
- Reads an image from Google Drive, and then displays it.

Link to the code in a python notebook: https://bit.ly/3IcuhFF

Note that the above code can be opened in GoogleColaboratory. To view python code in this notebook, you will need the Google Colaboratory plugin installed in the browser.

CODE

```python
[ ]  # Import opencv module to read and display images
     import cv2
     from google.colab.patches import cv2_imshow

     # Import gdown module to download files from google drive
     import gdown


[ ]  # Please change the url as needed (make sure you have the access to the file)
     url = "https://drive.google.com/file/d/1CokCuNkyP1zvuTXj_-hxIwevXz4TG9SA/view?usp=sharing"

     # Derive the file id from the url
     file_id = url.split('/')[-2]

     # Derive the download url of the file
     download_url = 'https://drive.google.com/uc?id=' + file_id

     # Give the file name you want to save it
     file_name = "dog.png"

     # Derive the file location
     file_location = "/content/" + file_name
```

Python Exercises

```
[ ]   # Download the file from drive
      gdown.download(download_url, file_location, quiet=False)

      # Read the image
      image = cv2.imread(file_location)

      # Output the image
      cv2_imshow(image)
```

Python Exercises

5. Data Visualization

What it does
 - Read CSV files from Google Drive, and plot histograms and bar plots of selected data columns

1. Histogram is plotted for a selected column

2. Bar graph is plotted for 2 columns

Link to the code in a python notebook: https://bit.ly/3LUlfzE

Note that the above code can be opened in GoogleColaboratory. To view python code in this notebook, you will need the Google Colaboratory plugin installed in the browser.

CODE

```
[ ]  # Import pandas module to read the CSV file and to process the tabular data
     import pandas as pd

     # Import matplotlib module for the data visualization
     import matplotlib.pyplot as plt

     # Import gdown module to download files from google drive
     import gdown

[ ]  # Please change the url as needed (make sure you have the access to the file)
     url = "https://drive.google.com/file/d/1J5z8OsAtgSp9i1eLxQFoxVexSZJuhI_-/view?usp=sharing"

     # Derive the file id from the url
     file_id = url.split('/')[-2]

     # Derive the download url of the file
     download_url = 'https://drive.google.com/uc?id=' + file_id

     # Give the file name you want to save it
     file_name = "child_vs_adult.csv"

     # Derive the file location
     file_location = "/content/" + file_name
```

Python Exercises

```
[ ]  # Download the file from drive
     gdown.download(download_url, file_location, quiet=False)

     # Read the CSV file
     data = pd.read_csv(file_location)


[ ]  # Print the details of the dataset including the column names.
     # You can use these details when selecting the column names for the following plots.
     print ('-------------- Details of the Dataset --------------')
     data.info()


[ ]  # Get the column names of the dataset
     column_names = data.columns

     # Select a column name to plot the hoistogram, after visualizing the details of the dataset.
     histogram_data = "years_school"

     # Get the data of the selected column
     x = data[histogram_data]

     # Plot the histogram (you can change the number of bins and the color as you needed)
     plt.hist(x, bins = 30, color = 'green')

     # Set the title, x-axis name and the y-axis name of the plot
     plt.title('Histogram for ' + histogram_data + 's')
     plt.xlabel('Number of ' + histogram_data + 's')
     plt.ylabel('Frequency')

     # Show the plot
     plt.show()
```

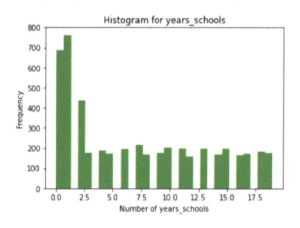

Plot the bar graph for selected columns

```
# Get a frequency count based on two columns
# Select the 2 column names, after visualizing the details of the dataset
data_bar = pd.crosstab(data.years_school, data.who_am_I)

# Plot the bar graph
bar_plot = data_bar.plot(kind='bar')

# Show the plot
plt.show()
```

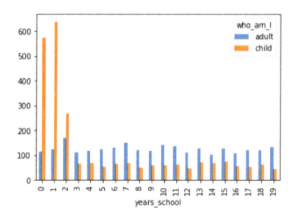

Teachers Corner

Core Concepts

In this chapter, students explore data - a critical component of any AI. The core concepts that students should appreciate are:

- Data is all around us
- Data comes in many different types - such as text, audio, video, numbers, etc.
- Understanding and selecting the right data is a critical part of building a good AI. Data analysis (where humans or other programs explore the data) is an important step before data is fed into an AI.
- Data needs to be transformed before it can be used in an AI. AIs only read numbers, so every type of data eventually becomes a series of numbers.
- AIs can understand complex data, but for real-world problems to be solved, humans need to understand at least part of the data. This is where data storytelling comes into play.
- Data analysis requires statistics and visualization.

Grade Level Alignment

The core concepts of data and its role in the AI life cycle are accessible to all grade levels in Middle School and High School. The data analysis section is more suitable for grades 7 and above. Students in grades 10 and above should already know the basic statistics - so teachers can focus on the application of these in Data Science.

The chapter also contains a series of Python examples. These are suitable for students with a working knowledge of Python, independent of grade level.

Some tips for discussions when teaching this chapter:

- Depending on your focus, you can decide whether to integrate the coding elements or not. For example - if you are focusing on STEM overviews or AI use in Science, then the coding exercises may not be necessary. If you are teaching AI as part of a Computer Science course, then we recommend the coding exercises.
- The coding exercises in this chapter are all in Python. They require the students to understand the following Python concepts
    - Input/Output
    - Modules

- Loops and Conditionals.
- Try/Catch error handling

If you need to teach these concepts, please see the curriculum listed below.

- There are many exercises that students can do offline (unplugged) that can help them appreciate how to analyze data. A simple exercise can be to ask them to note down what time they go to sleep every night. After about 2 weeks, they can analyze this data and see (a) does it differ between weeknights and weekends, and (b) what is the average time they go to bed.

Curriculum

Full curriculum covering chapters 1-10 is available at https://aiclub.world/teachers-material-book-volume-1

Curriculum for Unit 1 (Chapters 1-4) is available at https://aiclub.world/teachers-material-introduction-to-ai. Our teacher's curriculum include lesson guides, videos, presentation material, additional exercises, and assessments, as well as online support.

Scan the QR code for the Unit 1 curriculum (Chapters 1-4)

Scan the QR code for the teacher curriculum of this book

Assessment Key

Answer key to the assessment questions in the book can be found here: https://aiclub.world/teachers-material-introduction-to-ai

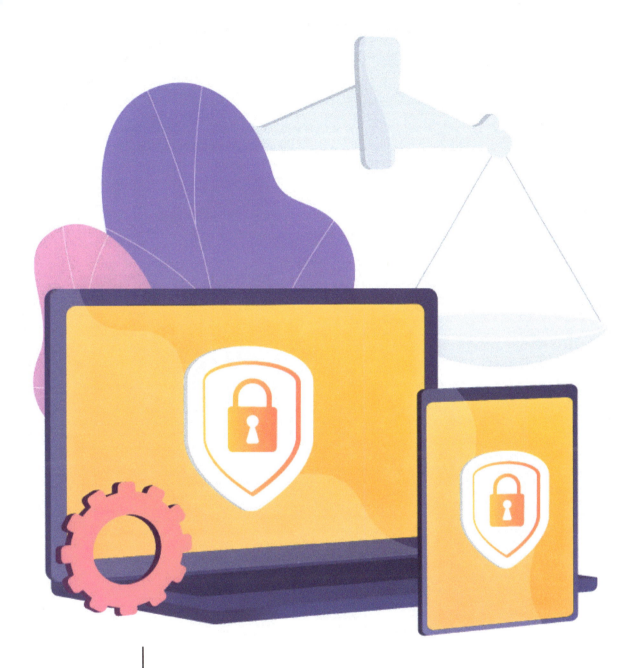

CHAPTER

4

AI Ethics I

As AI becomes more pervasive, its interaction with humans increases. AI is being used in everything from disease detection to loan approvals. As such, it becomes imperative that the technology, regardless of its promise, is developed in a safe way that protects humans and the planet. In short, AIs should behave in a way that reflects the values of the human societies that use the AIs. This chapter covers AI Ethics, a critical learning component for all students studying AI.

Context: Why should we care about AI Ethics?

Say that an AI tracks an individual's shopping habits and recommends foods for them to buy. Is that an acceptable use of their information? What if the same AI realizes that the individual has back pain (because they bought medicine), and their health insurance provider charges them more because the provider now knows that the person has back pain. Is that acceptable?

Say that an AI learns about a person from their social media history and a bank uses that information to deny the person a car loan because they think that he or she is not responsible. Is that ok?

As these examples show, AI has the ability to learn a lot about humans (sometimes even more than their friends or family know). Every person will have a different level of comfort about this. Hopefully these examples illustrate why societies and individuals should all care about AI Ethics.

Figure 4.1 Assessing the information on labels

What Makes AI Ethics Hard

While most humans and governments agree that AI Ethics is important, what exactly to do about it is a difficult problem. There are many reasons for this. The first is that not all humans agree on aspects of human ethics. For example - do all humans agree on what is fair? They do not. If some people get better opportunities than others - is that fair? Does it depend on the circumstance? Each human society has its own values, and these values often evolve with time. As such, it is difficult for an AI to *do what is right*, if humans cannot agree on what that is.

The second reason why AI Ethics is hard is that it is a multi-faceted topic. There are many aspects to AI Ethics. This chapter covers several of them
1. **AI Bias:** AI Bias is the area of AI Ethics focused on ensuring that AIs do not discriminate against minorities or under-represented populations.
2. **AI and Privacy:** Since AI relies upon data and information, a key focus is to ensure that AIs do not violate the privacy of the individuals that they learn about.
3. **Deepfakes and Misinformation:** AIs can create realistic-looking images,videos and other content that can be used for misinformation and fraud.
4. **AI and the Environment:** As larger and larger AIs get built, they consume massive amounts of computing resources. Ethics are needed to ensure that the impact on the environment is managed.
5. **AI and Access:** Virtually every country in the world now considers AI to be critical for staying competitive in the future. This means that countries that lack access to AI data or ways to train AI skills could get even further behind economically. Ethics are needed to ensure equitable access to AI technology and AI-powered resources.

AI Ethics is Everyone's Responsibility

Ensuring good AI Ethics is everyone's responsibility. So what can we all do?

Governments are starting to develop laws and guidelines to help corporations and others develop ethical AIs. These include
- Laws about how people's private information is used
- Laws about how AIs that affect people are monitored, reviewed and approved before they are used.

Both governments and public organizations are helping raise awareness of AI Ethics and why it matters.

Governments, corporations and public organizations are democratizing access to AI resources and datasets to help people in all countries develop AI competence.

What can individuals do? Every person can contribute to an ethical AI future by doing the following:
- Learn about AI Ethics (that is what this chapter is for!). This chapter covers each aspect of AI Ethics in turn. Each section examines the challenges of building ethical AIs and the best practices to apply when learning and practicing AI.
- Learn how to build safe and responsible AIs. See the exercises at the end of this chapter to develop hands on capabilities to build ethical AIs

Context: How to make AIs safe

Say that a school is using AI to decide what subjects students should learn. This AI has been trained on a lot of boys but does not know much about how girls learn. This AI then mistakenly decides that a girl is not good at math, because her learning pattern is not what the AI expects. Is this acceptable? Certainly not. But how can one ensure that this does not happen?

Figure 4.2 Student learning maths

Who needs to understand the AI and what do they need to know about the AI? Does the math teacher need to understand how the AI works? Does the school principal? If such an AI makes mistakes, how can a user tell? These are some of the challenges of building safe AIs that do not discriminate.

AI Bias

One of the most discussed aspects of AI Ethics is that of Bias - ensuring that AIs are not discriminating against minorities or other underrepresented groups. Discrimination can come in many forms. The most obvious example is if an AI approves benefits for some groups and not others (for example, if loans are approved for men but not women, or loans are approved for Caucasians but not African Americans where every other attribute is similar.) However, bias is not limited to granting of benefits. For example, if an AI trained to detect disease works with higher accuracy for some ethnic groups, that is also bias.

The first step to understanding how to prevent AI Bias is to understand how AI Bias can manifest.

How Bias Enters an AI

AIs are not natively biased. Bias is a human attribute that AIs can learn. As previous chapters have already covered, AIs learn from data. Through the data and the AI life cycle, AIs become structured to solve problems as defined by human creators. During an AI's creation, there are many points at which humans can inadvertently pass bias to an AI. They include Data, Problem Definition, and more.

Context: How Humans pass Bias to an AI

Take a moment to review the image in Figure 4.3. What does the image show? When this image was shown to large audiences, each individual saw different things in the image. Some believed it was a school graduation. Others thought it was a concert or picnic. Some thought it was a sporting event, and others thought it was a protest. This image is in fact of a protest in Ferguson, Missouri in the United States in 2017.

Figure 4.3 Assessing the information on labels

What this exercise illustrates is that, in the absence of information, every human brings their own perspective and interpretation to information. Since AIs lack perspectives of their own, they learn the perspectives passed on to them by their human creators.

The first step to mitigating AI Bias is to understand what bias we as humans are providing to the AIs that we create.

REFERENCE IMAGE SOURCE - https://www.facinghistory.org/resource-library/image/peaceful-protest-ferguson

AI Ethics

Bias in Data

Historical data is frequently biased, reflecting biases in human history that we do not want to see repeated. If historical data is given unmodified to the AI, the AI will learn these biases. For example, if an AI is trained with historical data of car loan approvals from the US, with all customer attributes including race and gender, that AI would likely learn that only middle-aged Caucasian men should get car loans. The AI will learn what was likely the historical approval pattern. To force the AI to consider *acceptable* attributes like credit rating or payment history, the AI's creators would need to explicitly exclude the attributes that they do not want to be considered.

Context: How AI Learns Bias from Data

Figure 4.4 shows a (fictional) dataset of car loan approvals. Visually examine this dataset. What patterns can be observed?

The first observation that most men have had their car loans approved. Very few approvals have gone to women and those to women of higher income. If this dataset is used to train an AI, what will it learn?

We trained an AI on this dataset and it decided that the gender of the applicant was the most important feature, and that income was less important. See Table 4.5 for the AI's priorities.

10195	Male	55	46017	Yes
10663	Male	60	42385	Yes
10074	Male	56	36325	Yes
10727	Male	59	49690	Yes
10991	Male	56	29793	Yes
10024	Male	45	29678	Yes
10693	Male	48	24018	Yes
10562	Male	51	29047	Yes
10986	Male	51	25328	Yes
10890	Male	35	28035	Yes
10132	Male	42	22863	Yes
10107	Male	39	28399	No
10872	Male	41	24507	No
10287	Male	41	23082	No
10853	Male	45	26204	Yes
10197	Male	38	20816	Yes
10408	Female	57	58977	Yes
10465	Female	54	53972	Yes
10113	Female	54	55257	No
10626	Female	57	58194	No
10661	Female	51	46593	No
10644	Female	60	45359	No
10690	Female	56	47136	No
10045	Female	39	41295	No
10986	Female	40	42783	No
10208	Female	36	47911	No
10331	Female	34	44002	No
10456	Female	42	46841	No

Figure 4.4

Figure 4.5 shows a table with each feature of the dataset and a number in the column Value that indicates how important the feature is. A large number indicates that the feature is relatively more important. As the table shows, the most important criteria the AI considers is whether the applicant is female. This is a clear case of bias.

Feature	Value
Gender_Female	0.32124965226699437
Income	0.2588797228196995
Age	0.17959562353982
Customer ID	0.1210632981736878
Gender_Male	0.11921170319979843

Figure 4.5

Bias in Problem Definition

Data is not the only way that bias can enter an AI. Another important area is problem definition. Note that AIs only solve the problem as it is defined by humans. They have no ability to expand the problem definition. For example, if a practitioner trains an AI to recommend the best teenager book for a user, it has no ability to recommend an adult book or elementary book. This is because it has been defined to not serve other user groups. If the human defining the problem believes the AI is not expected to serve a certain user group - it will by definition not be able to.

How does One Avoid Bias in Problem Definition?

- The key is to examine the problem definition and consider if this is the only way to state the problem or whether the human has added their own perspective of the problem.
- Note that, sometimes, adding human perspective is ok! For example, if a practitioner is an expert on the domain, they can make life easier for an AI by simplifying the problem. Lets take the example above. If the practitioner knows for sure that their customers want only teenager books, there is no need to confuse the AI by giving it options of elementary books or books for adults.
- Consider all the ways that the AI can be used and make sure the problem definition supports all the usage models.
- Once the AI is ready, it is important to give it to as many variants of the intended user group as possible. Then the practitioner can follow up with the users and ask them whether the AI gave them helpful answers. If the AI did not give helpful answers to a notable subset of the users, it is possible that a better problem definition will help.

Key things to know

Context

Most AIs do not have any perspective or *common sense* that humans have. There are researchers looking at ways to give AI common sense, but for now, remember that an AI only knows what it has learned from the data the human creator has given it.

An AI will take the shortest path to high accuracy. If that path runs through bias, or patterns in the data that humans are not even aware of, that pattern is what the AI is likely to discover and exploit. Sometimes these patterns may not even be visible to humans, but since AI algorithms specialize in pattern discovery, an AI can frequently discover hidden patterns that humans inspecting the data may not see.

Below is a very common illustration to help new AI practitioners understand how important it is to define the problem precisely and ensure that the AI understood the problem the way the human intended. Figure 4.6 shows 8 images of animals, 4 huskies (a type of dog) and 4 wolves. The AI was asked to distinguish between Husky and Wolf.

Examine the images. What distinguishing characteristics do you believe the AI learned?

The images framed in yellow are the AI's predictions for wolves, and the images framed in orange the prediction for huskies. The AI only got one prediction wrong - the one with the X. The AI predicted wolf when it should have been husky.

Figure 4.6 An AI distinguishing between a husky and a wolf

By examining the internals of the AI, it was discovered that the AI only learned to look for snow in the image and ignored the animals completely. The only mis prediction occurred because the husky was in snow. The critical item to note is the difference between the question that the human thought they were asking and the question the AI actually processed. For the human, naming the categories as Husky and Wolf has meaning. Since the human is aware these are both animals, our attention automatically goes to the animals. For the AI however the terms Husky and Wolf have no meaning, they are just character strings. The AI understood the question to be to determine what characteristics best distinguish the images (collections of pixels) in category 1 and the collections of pixels in category 2. It found the presence of snow to be the easiest distinguishing factor and did not need to consider other details to get a good accuracy.

Unexpected Manifestations of Bias

Given that AIs can learn bias, wouldn't the answer simply be to remove fields like race and gender from all datasets? Unfortunately, it is not quite so simple. There can be hidden patterns in data that humans may not be aware of, but that the AI will find. Those patterns can be biased. When these patterns are acceptable - we call them insights and this is in fact what we use AI for! However, when these patterns are not acceptable, we call them Bias and they need to be removed.

Context

Example: How race can manifest in unexpected ways

Figure 4.7 Conducting and taking part in an interview

Say that an AI designer wants to ensure that an AI that reviews resumes is not biased by an applicant's race. The first step would certainly be to ensure that the applicant's race is not listed anywhere in the resume. But is this enough?

Unfortunately, no. If the applicant's address is on the resume, it is very possible that, given people's nature to live in communities ethnically similar to their own, that an AI can find a correlation between an address and an ethnic group.

If the AI designer removes all addresses, is that enough? Unfortunately no. The school that the person went to, the state and country, can also indicate information about their ethnicity. Even if that is removed, the way the person chose to describe themselves in the resume, the language phrases used, etc. can indicate where they grew up or where they went to school.

As this example shows, removing patterns from data is very difficult. It is very possible for AIs to discover patterns in data that the humans were not even aware of. Given this, the task of mitigating bias is very challenging.

AI Ethics

Problems Caused by Bias

Bias in AI can do damage to both individuals and corporations. If a company is found to have created and used a biased AI - it can damage its reputation, cause customers to leave and cause other customers and employees to lose trust. People affected by the bias may even initiate lawsuits against the corporation. We have already seen how bias can affect individuals, by denying them benefits. Bias can also cause less visible damage. For example, if a digital assistant is trained on mostly voice data from one ethnic group, it is less likely to understand voice commands from customers with a different accent. The underrepresented customer group would get poorer service from the assistant and the company building the assistant would have a less competitive product among these groups.

Context

Example: Case Study - Tay Bot

In March 2016, Microsoft released a chatbot named Tay (Thinking About You) over Twitter. The chatbot was trained to interact with Twitter users. However, after only 16 hours (during which Tay had tweeted more than 96,000 times), Microsoft suspended the application due to inappropriate tweets generated by the bot. Theories abound as to what happened - including that Tay was purposefully attacked by malicious users or bots that exploited a vulnerability in the AI to teach it offensive content, or that the AI's creators did not sufficiently train it to understand what content was offensive in the first place.

Figure 4.8 Microsoft's Tay Chatbot

Regardless of the cause, the issues caused harm to Microsoft's reputation. The Daily Telegraph called Tay a "public relations disaster". The company issued an apology for Tay's controversial behavior and took the bot down. The incident also created wide concern about AIs and how well humans will be able to police AIs in the future.

REFERENCE SOURCE - https://www.telegraph.co.uk/technology/2016/03/25/we-must-teach-ai-machines-to-play-nice-and-police-themselves/

REFERENCE SOURCE - https://en.wikipedia.org/wiki/Tay_(bot)

NEWS & COMMENTARY

The Computer Got it Wrong: Why We're Taking the Detroit Police to Court Over a Faulty Face Recognition 'Match'

Face recognition technology turns everybody into a suspect and threatens our civil rights.

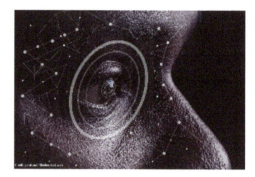

Figure 4.9 Newspaper article on facial recognition lawsuit

In April 2021, the American Civil Liberties Union (ACLU), jointly with other organizations, filed a federal lawsuit on behalf of an African American man, Robert Williams, who had been arrested by the Detroit police based on a faulty facial recognition match.

The lawsuit alleges that facial recognition has a long history of bias against minorities, and that the specific incident with Mr. Williams is the result of such AI Bias.

As AI becomes more prevalent, issues like this are particularly concerning for citizens and governments alike. As of early 2022, several cities and states across the United States have banned the use of facial recognition by their police departments.

REFERENCE SOURCE - https://www.aclu.org/news/privacy-technology/the-computer-got-it-wrong-why-were-taking-the-detroit-police-to-court-over-a-faulty-face-recognition-match/

Mitigating Bias

As already discussed, bias is a difficult problem to solve. The AIs themselves are not natively biased, but the skill that AI algorithms have in detecting patterns makes them particularly susceptible to learning bias from humans, whether from historical data or from unconscious biases in the humans that create the AIs. Bias mitigation is still an active area of research. Some of the common approaches being used today to mitigate bias include:

- Education: The first step is to make sure that everyone who creates or uses and AI is aware of AI's susceptibility to bias. This includes training data scientists and AI engineers to check data for sources of bias, and to review problem definitions to avoid bias.

- Testing: Real-world AI systems can be very complex, using thousands of features and millions or hundreds of millions of data samples. In such complex AIs, it is not possible to remove bias by inspection alone. A common practice is to test for bias, for example by providing the AI to many groups of users who differ in ethnic or similar attributes. If the AI behaves differently between these groups, it is likely that bias has crept in somewhere.

- Explainability: Some AI algorithms are capable of providing a rationale for their predictions. Such rationales are valuable to understand how the AI came to its decision and can be a very useful tool to fight bias. As such, some legally sensitive industries (such as Finance) are placing high importance on explainable algorithms and laws are starting to (at least implicitly) demand explainable algorithms in regulated industries. However, many AI algorithms are yet not explainable, so the challenge persists.

Context

Example: Legislation to mitigate bias

The United States Federal Trade Commission (FTC) is attempting to use existing consumer protection laws to regulate AI. Since these laws already prohibit unfair practices that target consumers based on ethnicity and such, the FTC is using them to prevent unexplainable algorithms from being used in industries governed by such laws.

Figure 4.10 Newspaper article on legislation to mitigate bias

REFERENCE SOURCE - https://searchenterpriseai.techtarget.com/feature/FTC-pursues-AI-regulation-bans-biased-algorithms

AI and Privacy

Another important area of AI Ethics is Privacy. AI thrives on data. Companies and governments are able to use AI to gather insights about people and behavior from data, thereby motivating them to gather even more data about people. As this cycle continues, both individuals and governments are expressing concern about the invasion of privacy. How much and what types of data are acceptable for use in an AI? Would an average individual know what information is being gathered about them and how it is being used to make decisions that affect them? What rights do individuals have to be informed about access to and use of information about their lives?

To illustrate this concern, consider the following scenarios
- In many countries, grocery stores offer a rewards program where a customer gets discounts on common items. In return, the customer is expected to use their rewards card for all purchases, implying that the store can now track purchasing habits for everyday goods. This information can be used by the store to determine if a customer is in ill health, if their hereditary patterns change, what desserts they like, etc. Some users will find this acceptable and others will not.
- In many countries, video cameras can be found in public spaces. Coupled with face recognition, these cameras can be used to track individuals as they walk down the street. In the hands of police, they can be used to investigate crimes.
- Digital assistants in our homes have AIs trained to respond to commands directed at them by names such as *"Hey Google" "Hey Alexa"* or *"Hey Siri"*. In order to detect their name, they must listen to every audio input in the vicinity and process it to look for their name. This implies that they are doing some processing on everything going on in the home they are in.
- Manufacturers of beds are now developing advanced bed technologies where sensors in the bed tracks human breathing sounds and uses AI to detect diseases such as a flu and cold before the user is aware of them. Some individuals will consider this a serious privacy violation.

Context

Case study: What does a mega store know about a user?

Let's do a hypothetical exercise. If a person buys clothing and everyday items from a store and also rents movies from them, or buys books from them, what could the store know about the customer? Below is a list of things the store could know.
- Customer's address (to ship the items)
- How many people live in a customer's house and their rough ages (if they buy clothes for everyone)
- Birthdays (if they buy party supplies at the same time every year)
- Whether the customer is losing weight (did their clothes' size change?)
- Whether the customer has back pain (did they buy over-the-counter painkillers?)
- The customer's relatives' addresses (if they were sent gifts?)
- What movies and books the customer likes
- Whether the family is expecting a new baby (buy baby books, diapers, baby toys?)
And more. These companies know a lot about their users.

Individuals have varying degrees of discomfort about privacy. For example, one person may feel that the use of a rewards card in a grocery store is acceptable while a bed tracking their sleep sounds is not. The challenges of privacy and AI come from this very fact - that there is no standard on what is acceptable. Because of this, each individual has a right to determine what they consider to be private, and then will need to determine if their sense of privacy has been violated. Many of the laws being proposed are about giving each individual that right.

Protecting Privacy in the Age of AI

There are several techniques that are now being used to protect a person's privacy in the age of AI. They include laws that govern how companies can use consumer information in algorithms. Great examples are the General Data Protection Regulation (GDPR) in the European Union, and the California Consumer Privacy Act (CCPA) in California in the United States. Such laws have provisions that not only regulate how customer data can be acquired, but also provide consumers with a "Right to Explanation". This implies that companies that use AIs that learn from consumer information may need to explain to customers how their data was used to make decisions and how each decision affected the customer.

Context

Case study: AI and the CCPA

At the time of this book's writing, the California Consumer Privacy Act (CCPA) is one of the most comprehensive pieces of legislation passed in the United States on behalf of consumer privacy. Similar legislation is occurring in other countries around the world. These laws have several important implications for AI:

Figures 4.11 Case study on CCPA

- Right to be informed: Consumers have a right to know what data about them is being used for.
- Right to deletion: If a consumer asks for data about them to be deleted, the company must do so.
- Right to Opt-Out: Consumers can ask for their data to be used for no other reason than whatever the business is. For example - if one ordered a book, the bookstore clearly needs to know that the customer ordered the book in order to deliver it. However, if the customer opted out, the bookstore should not use this information for any other reasons, like training an AI to recommend books to them or anyone else.

- Right of Access: Consumers should be able to access data about them.

To meet these requirements, companies have to carefully track all consumer information being used in an AI, and make sure all these requirements can be met.

Other techniques that can protect a user's privacy in the presence of AIs are:

- Anonymized data: This means that the customer cannot be identified in any way based on the information that the AI uses. A great example is medical data. Medical data (like MRI scans or XRays) are very useful for training AI's to detect diseases. There is no need for the patient's name to be included in the MRI information. The AI has no use for the name. By giving the patient an ID (like a number), it is possible to get useful data for an AI while protecting the user's privacy. If the dataset is more complex, more effort may be needed to anonymize it. For example, even if one deleted the user's name, if their birth date was kept, that could be enough to identify the user? In that case, it may be better keep the user's age when the data was taken, but not the date when the data was taken - so that the birth date cannot be derived.

- Synthetic data: Synthetic data is fake data. It may sound strange, but AIs are actually quite good at generating fake data! If one AI can generate data to train another AI, no user will even need to be involved. AIs are not the only way to generate synthetic data however. There are also statistical methods that can generate synthetic data.

- Differential Privacy: This is a method for creating datasets that contain useful information for AIs and other uses, but does not contain enough information to identify any individual user. For example, if the dataset contains statistics about a large user base, that could still be useful without exposing any individual and their details.

Case study: How AI Creates Synthetic Data!

Context

Oddly enough, the same AI techniques that can create realistic Deep Fakes can also create Synthetic Data! If an AI is given enough examples of, say, an X-Ray of people with COVID-19, it can learn how COVID-19 manifests in X-Rays. Once it knows this, it can create realistic-looking X-Rays for fictional COVID-19 patients. These images, in turn, can be used to train other AIs to detect COVID-19.

Figures 4.12 Case study AI and Synthetic Data

Till recently, the AIs that can generate these types of synthetic data (called Generative Adversarial Networks, or GANs) have been very expensive to train. However, with recent advances by companies such as NVidia and universities like MIT, these networks are becoming much cheaper to train effectively. This in turn can make Synthetic Data more of a reality.

REFERENCE SOURCE - https://medcitynews.com/2021/07/synthetic-data-a-new-solution-solving-historic-healthcare-privacy-challenges/

Case study: Synthetic Data for Self-driving Cars!

Self-driving cars create many privacy concerns. For example, self-driving cars need to use onboard cameras to *see* the road around them and make localized decisions. To train such an AI requires lots of images and video examples of road conditions. These can violate the privacy of any individual on the road.

Figure 4.13 Scenic road to drive on

Enter simulators! Rather than training the car's AI only on real pictures of roads, the AI can also be trained using simulators. Simulators can create realistic-looking images of any driving condition that the car needs to learn. In addition to protecting the privacy of real people on real roads, simulated road scenes have other advantages. The simulation can create any situation no matter how rare. For example, one can take real street videos for years and never come across a video of someone throwing paint at a car. However, with a simulation, creating visuals for this scenario is trivial!

REFERENCE SOURCE - https://apollo.auto/synthetic.html

Controlling Your Data in the Age of AI: Data Marketplaces

So far, this chapter has focused on the techniques that are being used to grant individuals either anonymity or greater visibility and control over how organizations use their personal data. The final item we will cover in AI and Privacy is the flip side of this effort. It is very clear that data has value and that AI can help extract that value. But who does the value belong to? Even if laws help an individual control what companies do with their data, one can argue that the private data is the property of an individual, and as such companies' use of it should not just be controlled, but rather that individuals should be compensated for the use of their data.

Enter data marketplaces. These are venues where individuals can sell their personal data, which is then aggregated into data products that corporations can purchase. Data marketplaces are growing rapidly as everyone realizes the value of data in the age of AI.

DeepFakes and Misinformation

The last section noted that AIs can generate Synthetic Data. The same types of AIs that create Synthetic data can also be used to create other types of Fakes. These are called Deep Fakes and can be used for many illegal purposes, such as misinformation and fraud.

Imagine if an AI can create a picture or a video of a human that is completely fake, but is very hard to distinguish from an actual picture or video of that person. What kinds of harm can this cause? It is possible that the fake video shows the person robbing a store. That video can be used to put the person in prison or ruin their reputation. Looking at it another way, if AIs can create fake videos or pictures that look very real, how do societies trust actual pictures and videos? If a store records a video of a person committing an actual robbery, the person can always claim that the video is fake.

These kinds of DeepFakes are becoming a serious problem for society. They can be used to create fake news, defraud people and companies, and incite violence. As AIs become more proficient at creating DeepFakes, technologists and researchers are also looking for more and more advanced ways to detect DeepFakes, also frequently using AI.

Case study: Which Person is Real?

Check out the pictures here. Which of these people are real?

It turns out none of them are! All of these faces are generated by an AI type called Generative Adversarial Neural Networks (or GANs).

Can one tell that the people are fake? Sometimes, if the pictures are closely examined, small details, like the symmetry of the eyes, can look off. Backgrounds, particularly if more than one person is in the picture, can look off. However, these AIs are getting better every day, so the fakes are becoming harder for humans to detect.

REFERENCE SOURCE - https://thispersondoesnotexist.com/

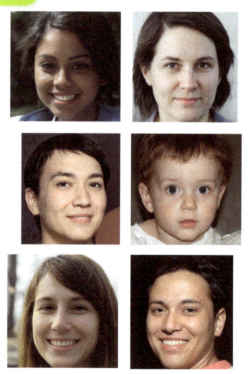

Figure 4.14 Samples or real and DeepFake images

Case study: Detecting Deep Fakes

A high school student built a novel website to detect Face Swaps, a type of DeepFake where the face of one person in a video is swapped with the face of a second person, making it seem as if the second person did whatever the first person did in the video.

This student built his AI by processing each image of the video with a Python library called BRISQUE. BRISQUE, which stands for Blind/Reference-less Image Spatial Quality Evaluator, is a set of techniques to assess image quality. By using a public dataset of real videos and face-swapped videos, he trained an AI to detect the image quality differences between real and fake videos. Users of his website can upload videos and the AI will use BRISQUE to evaluate the video image quality and decide whether it is fake. This app was a winner of the US Congressional App Challenge in 2021.

Figures 4.15 Screenshots of case study video

VIDEO LINK - https://youtu.be/kevJ0U3-XmE

How to Defend Against Deep Fakes

How does one defend against Deep Fakes? The first step is education. The more people know about Deep Fakes, the more likely it is that societies can defend against them. These days, just because a picture or video is posted, does not mean it is real. Supporting evidence is needed, now that humans know that AIs can generate very realistic-looking pictures and videos. Information sites, such as 'www.this-person-does-not-exist.com' help educate the general public about Deep Fakes.

The next step is to develop techniques to detect Deep Fakes. There are several such techniques that researchers have already developed. They include
- Training Neural Networks to tell the difference between Real and Fake images and videos
- Using image processing software to detect the quality of an image and using that to distinguish real and fake items. Real pictures and videos are naturally consistent in the symmetry of the human face, shadows and lighting, etc. Fake images and videos have to work hard to get these right. By looking for these details, one can sometimes tell the fakes apart.

Companies are also establishing challenges to educate the public and encourage everyone to develop solutions. A great example is the Kaggle DeepFake Detection Challenge of 2019, which offered $1 Million for the best DeepFake Detection solution.

REFERENCE SOURCE - https://www.kaggle.com/c/deepfake-detection-challenge

AI and the Environment

As companies and governments build even larger AI models, another ethics issue that arises is that of resource consumption. Some of the largest AI models in the world consume tremendous amounts of computing power every time that they train. The case study below is taken from a research paper that describes the computing power consumed by the largest language models in the world, in comparison to other human tasks such as a plane flight or driving a car. As the world battles climate change and tries to manage energy consumption, we also need to understand how much energy is being consumed by the AIs that we create.

Because of this issue, there are efforts underway to develop AI models that are more energy efficient. While many AI algorithms focus on creating models that have the highest possible predictive performance (such as accuracy), researchers are now developing AI algorithms that generate almost as much accuracy but do so with much less computing power. An example is DistilBERT from Hugging Face, which is 40% smaller than its full energy counterpart, yet up to 97% as effective on certain prediction tasks. These types of models can also be useful for other reasons. For example, AIs that are energy efficient can be used in mobile phones, sensors, or other locations where large amounts of compute are not available.

 Context

Case study: Carbon Emissions of Large Language AIs

How much CO2 does a large AI generate? As we know, AIs need to be trained, and many AIs do not train just once. They need to be trained multiple times with tuning to get the best performance. Even after the best performance is achieved, the AI may still need to be retrained if new data is available.

As the table shows, training a large AI can generate as much as five times as much CO2 as one car consumes in its lifetime, and twenty times as much CO2 as an average American generates in a lifetime. As the world tries to cut down carbon emissions, AIs are clearly a place to focus on.

Everyday tasks	CO2 generated (in lbs)
One person flying from New York to San Francisco	1,984
Average person in one year	11,023
Average American in one year	36,156
Average car in its lifetime	126,000
AI tasks (Natural Language Processing)	
Training one AI with a GPU (with tuning and experimentation)	78,468
Creating one Large NLP Transformer with Neural Architecture Search	626,155

Figure 4.16 CO2 generation in lbs

DATA TAKEN FROM REFERENCE SOURCE - https://arxiv.org/pdf/1906.02243.pdf

AI Ethics

Context

DistilBERT, a distilled version of BERT: smaller, faster, cheaper and lighter

Victor SANH, Lysandre DEBUT, Julien CHAUMOND, Thomas WOLF
Hugging Face
{victor,lysandre,julien,thomas}@huggingface.co

Figure 4.17

Here are some examples of energy efficient AIs created by different companies over the last decade.

The first one is DistilBERT, a natural language understanding (NLU) model. Based on the very popular BERT (Bidirectional Encoder Representations from Transformers) model series, DistilBERT was published by Hugging Face in 2019. Its researchers demonstrated that DistilBERT achieves 97% of the performance of a regular BERT model for GLUE - a public language understanding benchmark, while being 40% smaller and 60% faster.

More details about DistilBERT can be found here: https://arxiv.org/pdf/1910.01108.pdf

MobileNetV2: Inverted Residuals and Linear Bottlenecks

Mark Sandler   Andrew Howard   Menglong Zhu   Andrey Zhmoginov   Liang-Chieh Chen
Google Inc.
{sandler, howarda, menglong, azhmogin, lcchen}@google.com

Figure 4.18

Other energy efficient AIs include MobileNetV2 from Google. Introduced in 2018, MobileNetV2 (a follow-up to its precursor MobileNet), focuses on energy efficient Convolutional Neural Networks (CNNs). Google has demonstrated that MobileNetV2 can be efficient for many tasks from image classification to object detection.

DATA TAKEN FROM REFERENCE SOURCE - https://arxiv.org/pdf/1801.04381.pdf

AI and Data Access

Another area of concern among AI Ethicists is data access. As discovered in previous chapters, AI thrives on data. As companies and governments race to get an edge in AI, those with the most data have an advantage. As AI usage grows, what can societies do to ensure that some countries are not left behind due to a lack of data? Or should the world allow competition to occur naturally and let those who win,win?

Like most of the AI Ethics issues explored in this chapter, opinions vary and there is no established right answer. Efforts are being made by large corporations to provide open access to datasets for critical problems - such as DeepFakes. Public datasets encourage wide innovation on new AI technologies from anywhere in the world. Data marketplaces, as covered earlier in this chapter, are another effort to give individuals more direct control over who profits from their personal information and create ways for data to be more widely accessible. Simulations and synthetic data are another way to create more data, hopefully in ways that enable everyone to benefit. However, even with such efforts, lack of data still remains a barrier to entry for many. For example, startup companies looking to innovate and compete with mainstream players and smaller nations looking to compete with more industrialized counterparts all struggle with the lack of data.

As AI use explodes, one would expect to see more laws governing data access, for both privacy and competitive reasons.

AI Ethics - A Global Responsibility

Ensuring good AI Ethics is everyone's responsibility. So what can we all do?

- Learn about AI Ethics (that is what this chapter is for!).
- Learn how to build safe and responsible AIs. See the exercises at the end of this chapter to develop capabilities to build ethical AIs
- Share knowledge with others! AI is a great opportunity, but whether it turns out to be a benefit or a problem for humanity will depend on all of us and how we manage, guide and shape AI.

In 2021 the United States created an initiative to provide generally accessible computing resources and open datasets to enable researchers to advance in AI. This group has been tasked with ways to support infrastructure and other resources to develop AI competency across individuals of all ages, from students to professionals. This is the most recent US initiative as of the writing of this book. More details can be found at https://www.ai.gov/

Similar initiatives have been launched in countries around the world. Canada was one of the first, adopting a national AI strategy in 2017 and driving AI innovation hubs around the nation (https://cifar.ca/ai/). China has taken similar steps (https://link.springer.com/article/10.1007/s00146-020-00992-2). Many nations perceive leadership in AI as critical for being competitive in the global marketplace.

HOME / PAN-CANADIAN AI STRATEGY

Pan-Canadian AI Strategy

ADVANCING AI

CIFAR is fuelling AI research and innovation.

In 2017, the Government of Canada appointed CIFAR to develop and lead a $125 million Pan-Canadian Artificial Intelligence Strategy, the world's first national AI strategy.

CIFAR works in close collaboration with Canada's three national AI Institutes — Amii in Edmonton, Mila in Montreal, and the Vector Institute in Toronto, as well as universities, hospitals and organizations across the country.

Figure 4.19

Assessment

1. Which of the following are parts of AI Ethics?
(a) Maintaining privacy (b) Removing bias (c) Improving human trust in AI (d)Detecting and removing DeepFakes (e) All of the above

2. Which of the following are good examples of being Ethical with AI?
(a) Making sure that the AI can explain its decisions (b) Making sure that the AI has the highest accuracy (c) Making sure that the AI predicts correctly every time (d) Making sure that the AI only uses public data (e) All of the above

3. Why should we be concerned about AI's impact on the environment?
(a) AIs can classify trash as recyclable or not (b)AIs consume a lot of computing power and that can cause carbon emissions (c) AIs can replace some jobs done today by humans (d) AIs can create new applications - like self-driving cars (e) All of the above

4.You are responsible for an AI that will decide whether a bank's customers are approved for car loans. Which of the following would be good practices to make sure the AI is not biased?
(a) Use an explainable algorithm and check its decision process to make sure you are comfortable with the customer information that the AI is using to make its decisions
(b) Ask each customer to tell you whether they think the AI is biased (c) Make sure the AI approves every loan (d) Make sure that only public data is used to train the AI (e) All of the above

5.What is a Deep Fake?
(a) An image, video, or other artifacts that looks real but is not (b) An image, video, or other artifacts that is created by an AI (c) An AI that is trained from fake images (d) An AI that is used to detect whether an image is fake (e) All of the above

6. How can we test whether an AI is biased?
(a) Measure its accuracy (b) Measure its confusion matrix (c) Measure its Root Mean Square Error (d) Test it against different samples and see if you are comfortable with the results (e) Only use an explainable algorithm

AI Ethics

7. How do we combat AI-created disinformation?
(a) Educate the public to be skeptical about evidence and ask questions (b) Educate the public on the telltale signs of deep fakes (c) Build AIs to detect deep fakes (d) Confirm facts through multiple independent sources (e) All of the above

8. You are responsible for building an AI that will select whether a college applicant should be admitted to a particular university. You are using historical data on previous applicants to train your AI. How can bias possibly enter your AI?
(a) The university may previously have discriminated against certain applicants, in which case the historical data will reflect that. (b) The dataset may not be enough to create a high accuracy AI (c) You may not use the algorithm that created the highest accuracy AI because you did not know that algorithm existed (d) You may build the AI with the wrong programming language. (e) All of the above

9. Which stages of the AI life cycle can bias enter?
(a) Problem definition (b) Data (c) Training (d) Deployment (e) All of the above

10. Who is responsible for making sure that an AI does not have a bias?
(a) The person who selected the data (usually a data scientist) (b) The person who defined the problem (possibly a product manager) (c) The person who wrote the code (possibly a machine learning engineer) (d) All of the above (1-3) (e) None of the three (1-3)

Online Activities

1. Facial Recognition Ban

Do a Google search and find 5 cities around the world that have banned the use of Facial Recognition by police. Why did the cities do this?

2. Build an AI

In this activity, two AIs are build, one using images and another using tabular data. Follow the QR code attached at the end or simply go to https://aiclub.world/ai-ethics to start this activity!

(a) Image Classification

In this activity, an AI to classify between two types of fruits from images is built. This is used to demonstrate how an AI trained for a specific task cannot say *I don't know* which can have ethical impact in more serious applications in the real world.

In this activity, we will learn
• What is the accuracy of the AI
• Try and see how it works for images of apples and bananas
• Try a picture of an orange - what does the AI think it is and why
• What does this have to do with Ethics

(b) Build an AI and Detect Bias

In this activity, an AI is built to advise the penitentiary system whether an inmate up for parole is likely to re-offend.

In this activity, we will learn
• How to check for *Bias*
• Ways to mitigate bias
• Does gender qualify as bias in this case

Scan for - https://aiclub.world/ai-ethics

Unplugged Activities

Exercise 1 - What is in this image

Take a look at this image - what do you think this image is about?

Ask your friends - what is this image about?

Answer:

This image is from a protest in a United States city called Ferguson. However, while some may think this is a protest, others may think it is a concert, people on their way to a picnic, a school graduation, etc.

What have we learned?
Human perspective on the same information varies widely. This is one reason why it is so hard for AIs to be "fair" or any other such term that means different things to different people. If humans cannot agree on what the right answer is - we cannot expect the AI to get it "right" either

Unplugged Activities

Exercise 2

We work for a bank and we want to build an AI that can help a bank decide whether or not to give a loan to a customer. We will train our AI using data from past customers. The data we have is in the table below

Gender	Age	Income	Yes or No on Loan
Male	20	2000	No
Male	20	10000	Yes
Male	50	15000	Yes
Female	20	2000	No
Female	20	10000	No
Female	50	15000	No

Answer the following questions

1. What do the customers who got loans have the most in common?

2. If we train an AI with this data, who is likely to not get a loan? Is this ok?

Unplugged Activities

Exercise 3

How about if we change the data to remove one column and remove all data about female customers. Now the data looks like this

Age	Income	Yes or No on Loan
20	2000	No
20	10000	Yes
50	15000	Yes

Answer the following questions

1. What do the customers who got the loans now have in common?

2. Who is now not likely to get a loan? Is this ok?

Exercise 4

Please review the Google standard for AI Ethics (as assessed in December 2021). Write your own AI Ethics mission statement. What would you do differently?

Scan the QR code to read more from https://ai.google/principles/

RESPONSIBILITIES ›

Artificial Intelligence at Google: Our Principles

Google aspires to create technologies that solve important problems and help people in their daily lives. We are optimistic about the incredible potential for AI and other advanced technologies to empower people, widely benefit current and future generations, and work for the common good.

Scan for -https://ai.google/principles/

Unplugged Activities

Exercise 5

Answer the following questions about yourself
1. Do you trust AIs?
2. If yes - why?
3. If no - why?
4. If you do not trust AIs - what would the creator of an AI need to do to make it possible for you to trust it?
5. If you do trust AIs - is there anything that can happen that may cause you to lose your trust in the AI?

You own a bookshop and you would like to build an AI to recommend books to your customers. Below is a table of different customers and what they have bought first and second. That normal has changed, and some are no longer working as they should.

Teachers Corner

Core Concepts

AI Ethics is a critical aspect of AI that individuals everywhere, particularly middle school and high school students, should learn. By the end of this chapter, students should be able to:
- Appreciate that there are many ways that AI intersects with human life and with businesses
- Understand and describe the need for Ethical practices in AI
- Understand and describe the technical aspects of AI that cause challenges

Grade Level Alignment
This chapter is appropriate for any middle school or high school grade level.

Teachers Corner

Tips

Depending on the focus of your classroom, you may decide to teach the AI Ethics chapter right after Chapter 1 (What is AI). This combination is appropriate for any class where an in-depth exploration of AI is not planned.

Additional discussions that can help students explore the topic

- Explore the ethical aspects of other technologies - like Nuclear Power. Are there similarities? For example - Nuclear technology has created both power plants that power entire cities, and bombs that can kill millions. Was that a technology decision or a human one? How is the human race trying to manage this technology? Will we need similar actions for AI?
- When an AI makes a mistake, who is responsible? What if a self-driving car kills someone? Who is responsible?
- AIs learn bias from data and from humans. All humans are biased in some form. How is a biased AI more damaging? Is it because we don't understand the bias and do not know how to evaluate it?

Curriculum

Full curriculum covering chapters 1-10 is available at https://aiclub.world/teachers-material-book-volume-1
Curriculum for Chapter 4 is available at https://aiclub.world/teachers-material-ethics. Our teacher's curriculums include lesson guides, videos, presentation material, additional exercises, and assessments, as well as online support.

Scan the QR code for the Unit 1 curriculum (Chapters 1-4)

Scan the QR code for the teacher curriculum of this book

Assessment Key
Answer key to the assessment questions in the book can be found here: https://aiclub.world/teachers-material-ethics

Classification

Artificial Intelligence services can perform several different types of tasks. Classification is the name given to AIs that predict a class (a category). In this chapter, several examples are used to understand the classification type of AI.

What is Classification?

Classification is a type of AI where the AI predicts a category. A category can be *Good* vs *Bad*, *Hot* vs *Cold,* etc. It does not matter what the input to the AI (the question) was. The input data can be numbers, categories, text, images, any combination of these, or anything else. It is only the format of the answer - the prediction - that determines whether the AI problem is Classification.

Figure 5.1

Concept

Binary Classification

When there are only two classes (categories) to predict, it is called Binary Classification

Classification can predict more than 2 categories. When there are only two categories, it is called *Binary Classification*. When there are more than two, it is called *Multi-Class Classification*.

Classification

Binary Classification   Multi-Class Classification

Classification is a type of supervised learning since the number of categories and the names of each category have to be known by the AI before it can learn the pattern and learn how to map questions to one of the category values as an answer. Figure 5.2 shows an example classification dataset. In this dataset, the AI will learn how to classify a person as an *Adult* or a *Child* based on three pieces of information: the number of countries this person has visited, the number of years they have spent in school, and their height.

Classification can be done with virtually any type of data. The only factor that determines whether an AI is of type classification is the prediction label, which must be category. If this is true, no matter what the input (features), it is a classification problem.

Number of Countries Visited	Number of Years in School	Height (Feet)	Original Label Who am I?
15	13	5.0	Adult
2	3	3.5	Child
7	4	4.0	Child
1	5	7.0	Adult

Figure 5.2 Example dataset

Classification with Numerical and Categorical Data

Figure 5.3 shows an example of classification with numerical and categorical data. In this case, a bank is trying to determine whether a customer is likely to stay with the bank or leave and close the account. As you can see from the table, there are many features, some numerical and some categorical. The numerical features include the customer's age, bank balance, and income. The categorical features include whether they have a credit card (1->Yes, 0->No), whether they are married (1->Yes, 0->No), and whether they have kids (1->Yes, 0->No). The label is the column *Exited*, where the value 1 indicates that they are likely to leave and 0 indicates they are not likely to leave. The categorical label determines the type of AI.

CreditScore	Age	Tenure	Balance	NumOfProducts	HasCrCard	IsActiveMember	EstimatedSalary	Exited
619	42	2	0	1	1	1	101348.88	1
608	41	1	83807.86	1	0	1	112542.58	0
502	42	8	159660.8	3	1	0	113931.57	1
699	39	1	0	2	0	0	93826.63	0
850	43	2	125510.82	1	1	1	79084.1	0
645	44	8	113755.78	2	1	0	149756.71	1
822	50	7	0	2	1	1	10062.8	0
376	29	4	115046.74	4	1	0	119346.88	1
501	44	4	142051.07	2	0	1	74940.5	0
684	27	2	134603.88	1	1	1	71725.73	0
528	31	6	102016.72	2	0	0	80181.12	0
497	24	3	0	2	1	0	76390.01	0
476	34	10	0	2	1	0	26260.98	0
549	25	5	0	2	0	0	190857.79	0
635	35	7	0	2	1	1	65951.65	0
616	45	3	143129.41	2	0	1	64327.26	0
653	58	1	132602.88	1	1	0	5097.67	1
549	24	9	0	2	1	1	14406.41	0
587	45	6	0	1	0	0	158684.81	0

Figure 5.3 Example classification dataset with categorical and numerical features

Classification with Text Data

Figure 5.4 shows an example of classification with text data. In this case the feature is an English text (which can be anything from a single character to many sentences), and the prediction is *Happy* or *Sad*.

feeling	sentence
sad	I am so sad to see you go.
happy	I am so excited for tomorrow!
sad	It burns me up
happy	Mom and dad are planning a great party for christmas. I am excited
happy	We don't have school tomorrow!
sad	my pet died
sad	Why does school have to start so early?

Figure 5.4 Example classification dataset

Classification with Image Data

Figure 5.5 shows an example of classification with image data. In this case, the feature is the image itself, and the prediction is the category *Cat* or *Dog*.

Note that many data types can be combined as well. For example, it is possible (and common) to have structured data where some columns are categories, some are numbers, and some are text.

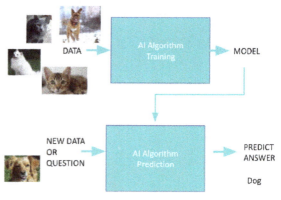

Figure 5.5 Training and Prediction

How is Classification Measured?

As noted in Chapter 2, supervised learning algorithms are measured by splitting the data into a training set and a validation set. The training set is used to train the AI and the validation set is used to test the AI. This approach is taken since classification is a supervised learning problem. This section describes exactly how the validation set is used to test a classification AI and some of the metrics used to measure classification performance.

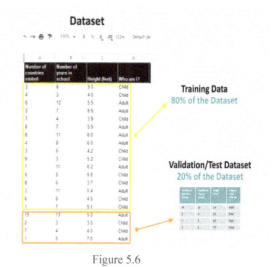

Figure 5.6

Context — Spam filtering in Gmail

Spam in emails had become a major issue and led to the emergence of algorithms that would automatically classify emails into spam and prevent them from crowding your inbox. Google used sophisticated AI algorithms (neural networks) to identify emails as spam. The results show that Gmail is able to catch 99.9 percent of the spam emails successfully. Achieving high accuracy here is important to ensure the user's inbox is not flooded with junk emails. At the same time, the user should not miss an important email because of misclassification.

Accuracy

The most basic and common measure of a classification AI is accuracy. Figure 5.7 shows how accuracy works. Each row of the validation dataset is submitted to the AI and its response is compared to the correct answer already available in the validation set. The accuracy is the number of correct answers divided by the total number of questions. The highest possible accuracy is 100% (if the AI got all predictions right) and the lowest is 0% (if the AI got all predictions wrong).

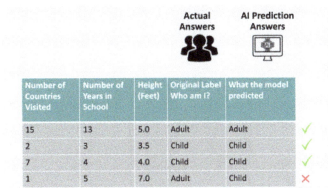

Number of Countries Visited	Number of Years in School	Height (Feet)	Original Label Who am I?	What the model predicted	
15	13	5.0	Adult	Adult	✓
2	3	3.5	Child	Child	✓
7	4	4.0	Child	Child	✓
1	5	7.0	Adult	Child	✗

Figure 5.7 Example of accuracy calculation

What constitutes good accuracy? It is extremely situation dependent. For example, if the AI is used to predict whether an aircraft will crash, or whether a person has cancer, even a 95% accuracy is likely not good enough - since it implies a 5% chance of a life-threatening outcome. On the other hand, if the AI is used to predict whether a service is good or bad - even a 85% accuracy is great. Accuracy provides a quantified metric of performance. How it is interpreted is a matter of human judgment.

Flaws in Accuracy

Accuracy is not a perfect metric. Consider the two scenarios in Figure 5.8 where the AI is predicting between *Adult* and *Child*. In each case the correct answer is in column *True Label* and the AI's prediction is in column *Predicted Value*. The AI on the left has an accuracy of 60% and the AI on the right has an accuracy of 80%. If only the accuracy metric is inspected, the AI on the right would be deemed superior. However, a closer examination of the tables shows that the AI on the right never predicts *Adult*. So why did it get a higher accuracy?

True Label	Predicted Value
Adult	Adult
Adult	Child
Child	Adult
Adult	Child
Child	Child
Child	Child
Child	Adult
Adult	Adult
Child	Child
Adult	Adult

True Label	Predicted Value
Child	Child
Child	Child
Child	Child
Adult	Child
Child	Child
Child	Child
Child	Child
Adult	Child
Child	Child
Child	Child

Figures 5.8 Two tables showing predictions made by two AIs

The AI on the right got a higher accuracy because the validation dataset had only two examples of Adult (20%). Since the validation dataset was selected randomly from the dataset, this suggests that the original dataset was heavily skewed and likely had very few examples of *Adult*. When such skew occurs, the accuracy metric can be misleading.

Skew is unfortunately a common issue in real-world datasets since all the categories that the AI is expected to predict are unlikely to occur with equal frequency.

Confusion Matrix

While accuracy is a useful metric, it is often insufficient to fully understand the AI's behavior. To provide more insight, there is a second metric, Confusion Matrix. Figure 5.9 shows the confusion matrix for the first table in Figure 5.8.

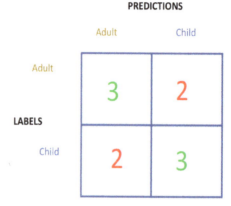

Figures 5.9 Confusion matrix example

The confusion matrix contains one row and one column for every category being predicted. As such, a binary classification problem would have a 2x2 confusion matrix (2 rows and 2 columns). A classification problem with 5 categories would have 5 rows and 5 columns, and so on. Each row represents all the examples in the validation dataset for which the answer is that category. Each column represents what the AI predicted. For example, in Figure 5.9, you can see that the validation dataset contained 5 examples of *Child* and 5 examples of *Adult*. In each case, the AI got 3 correct (3 *Child* correct and 3 *Adult* correct) and 2 wrong.

Data Skew in Real Life

Artificial Intelligence algorithms are being used in medical diagnosis to assist doctors in making diagnosis. For example, an AI can be trained to recognize patterns of cancer cells from pathology images of biopsies. One thing to note here is that datasets that are used for training these AIs will typically have more examples of healthy patients than the ones with cancer since most biopsies come back with a negative result. It is the responsibility of the data scientist to take into account the skew in data and inspect the confusion matrix along with accuracy to ensure the AI does not miss patients with cancer. If an AI mispredicts someone having cancer as healthy, it directly impacts the life of an individual and hence care is taken that only the AIs with perfect diagnostic score for the cancerous category are used in real life.

The accuracy can be calculated from the confusion matrix. Just add up all of the numbers on the diagonal and divide by the sum of all the numbers in the entire matrix. As we noted before, the accuracy was 60%.

So, how does the confusion matrix provide more insight into the behavior of the AI? Figure 5.10 shows the confusion matrix of the second AI. In studying this, several concerns are apparent. First, the numbers on each row are not even and the validation set contained far more *Adult* examples than *Child* examples. Second, the *Child* column is entirely zeros, indicating that this AI has not demonstrated an ability to predict *Child* no matter what the correct answer was. Even though the accuracy is 80%, we can see that this is an inferior AI.

PREDICTIONS

	Adult	Child
Adult	0	2
Child	0	8

LABELS

Figures 5.10

False Positives and Negatives, True Positives and Negatives

When the classification is a binary classification (two categories), there are several other terms that are used that you should know. These are very common when AI is used to diagnose diseases, for example.

One of the two categories is called the Positive, and the other the Negative. For example, if your AI is diagnosing cancer, Positive will be that you have cancer. True Positive means that the correct answer is Positive and the AI predicted Positive. False Positive means that the correct answer is Negative and the AI predicted Positive.

While True Positives and True Negatives are always good, False Positives and False Negatives are not equally bad. In many cases where AI is used to diagnose diseases, a False Negative can be far more harmful than a False Positive. A False Negative by an AI can send a sick patient home where they may get sicker. A False Positive, while it may cause stress, is less harmful since it will likely be followed by more medical tests which will prove that the AI made a mistake.

Characteristics of a Good Classification AI

Now that we know how to measure an AI, what are the characteristics that we should be looking for to determine whether our AI is good at its job?

The first is high accuracy. Note that if your AI is predicting between two categories and its accuracy is 50%, that is the same as a random guess! If its accuracy is less than 50%, then taking the opposite answer from what your AI predicts is actually the better choice! As long as the accuracy is greater than 50%, at least the AI has learned something. From then on - higher accuracy is better. You can use the same logic for more than 2 categories. For example, if the AI is predicting between three categories, 33% (or 100/3) is as good as a random guess.

Once the AI has learned something and is not randomly guessing, one has to apply human judgment to decide whether the accuracy is good enough. For example, a 60% accuracy is likely not good no matter what the problem is. 85% accuracy on the other hand, is good for many problems like recommending books, where the consequences of a wrong answer are not too bad. In medical usage, or any other situation where a wrong answer can hurt people, 85% will not be acceptable, and values of 95% or greater will likely be required.

Activity

If an AI is predicting 4 categories (a) Happy (b) Neutral (c) Annoyed and (d) Angry, with an accuracy of 23.5%, is that better than random prediction?
How about if the accuracy was 50%?

The next thing to ensure is that your AI is able to predict all of the categories correctly (or at least satisfactorily). Confusion matrix can be inspected to confirm this. It should be confirmed that the AI is not getting a high accuracy score just because the questions are skewed and not testing all categories. How good is good enough again depends on human judgment. It may be more important to get some categories right than others. It is decided based on the problem (think about the example earlier about positive vs negative detection in cancer).

Activity

If an AI is predicting 4 categories (a) Happy (b) Neutral (c) Annoyed and (d) Angry, the confusion matrix is shown below:

	Happy	Neutral	Annoyed	Angry
Happy	30	5	26	4
Neutral	22	23	35	2
Annoyed	3	4	5	1
Angry	1	3	21	35

(i) Calculate the accuracy of this AI.
(ii) Would you consider this a satisfactory AI?

Once the AI can predict all the categories well enough for the problem, it can be confirmed to be a good AI!

Common Classification Algorithms

There are many AI algorithms that can perform classification. Some are listed below
- Decision Trees (covered later in this book)
- K Nearest Neighbors (covered later in this book)
- Neural Networks (covered later in this book)
- Logistic Regression (covered in the Advanced AI book)
- Support Vector Machines (covered in the Advanced AI book)

What do these algorithms have in common? They are all able to find patterns in the input data that separate different categories. Metrics of accuracy and confusion matrix are used to decide if each algorithm is doing a good job predicting the label categories in the data. These metrics can be used to compare different algorithms and select the best one.

What makes these algorithms different? They are all different approaches, and each has its advantages and disadvantages. For example - Decision Trees and K Nearest Neighbor are Explainable, which means that they can provide humans with a description of how they arrived at their prediction decision. This can be very useful when your AI is in a field where the company using it can get sued, or where we want to make sure that the AI is applied fairly and does not make biased decisions. Neural Networks on the other hand are great for complex data (like deciding whether a picture contains a cat or a dog), but are much harder to explain.

AI in Agriculture
Context

Artificial Intelligence algorithms are being used in agriculture to inspect plants for diseases. For example, an AI can look at the picture of a tomato plant and classify it as (a) Healthy (b) Early Blight (c) Late Blight (d) Septoria or (d) Curl Virus. Such an AI helps farmers use automation for recognition of plant diseases. This helps them take steps early and prevent further damage to the crop. You can read more about this project here: https://www.corp.

aiclub.world/post/the-success-of-tomato-genius

Assessment

1. What is the difference between binary and multi-class classification?

2. List the data type constraints on features for a task to qualify as a classification problem?

3. How is the performance of a classification AI measured?

4. If an AI predicted 47 questions correctly out of 61 questions that it was asked, what is its accuracy value?

5. If an AI has the following confusion matrix, what is its accuracy?

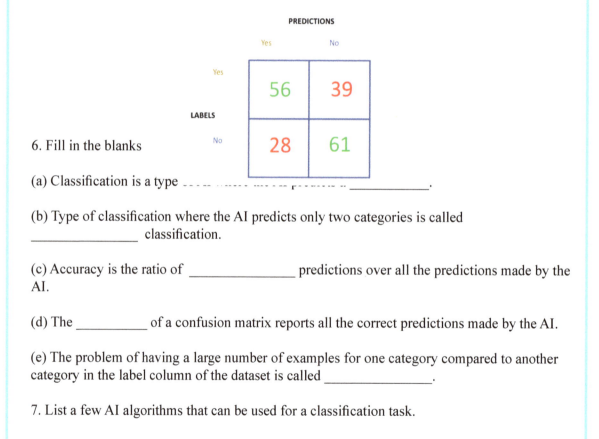

6. Fill in the blanks

(a) Classification is a type _____.

(b) Type of classification where the AI predicts only two categories is called _____ classification.

(c) Accuracy is the ratio of _____ predictions over all the predictions made by the AI.

(d) The _____ of a confusion matrix reports all the correct predictions made by the AI.

(e) The problem of having a large number of examples for one category compared to another category in the label column of the dataset is called _____.

7. List a few AI algorithms that can be used for a classification task.

Assessment

8. If an AI reports a validation accuracy of 85% and the training dataset has 500 samples, where 20% of the samples are kept aside for validation, how many samples did the AI predict correctly to achieve the accuracy of 85%?

9. A training dataset contains 3 categories in its label column: happy, neutral and sad. Would it be possible to calculate the confusion matrix? How many rows and columns would the matrix have? Please explain.

10. If the label column of a dataset has 2 categories, where one category has 500 examples and the other one has 100 examples, how would you measure the performance of the AI? Please explain.

11. Explain the term skew in the context of a training dataset.

12. Calculate the accuracy and confusion matrix for the below table.

Gender	Feeling	Mood	Prediction
Male	jumping with joy	Happy	Happy
Female	headache	Sad	Sad
Female	holidays, yay!	Happy	Sad

13. Why is classification a type of supervised learning? Please explain.

14. In a binary classification problem, which of the following terms indicate correct predictions by the AI (a) True Positive (b) True Negative (c) False Positive (d) False Negative

15. How does the Confusion Matrix provide more insight into the behavior of the AI?

Online Activities

1. Can a Classification AI understand Language?

In this activity, we will do simple exercises to understand if an AI is smart enough to understand languages. Please go to https://aiclub.world/activity-ai-languages to start this activity!

In this activity, we will learn
• If AI can understand language
• If AI can convert audio signals into words in a language
• If AI can make predictions based on its understanding of language
• How to build an AI for sentiment analysis

This activity has an interactive component where students will enter different sentences and the AI will predict if it is a happy or sad sentiment

To do the interactive activity, you will need a computer with a chrome browser.

Python Exercises

Python code is provided in this module to help students get hands-on experience interacting with concepts covered in the chapter. The code snippets are kept simple and self-contained. All the code included in this book is available in a GitHub repository https://github.com/pyxeda/MiddleSchoolCurriculum/tree/master/Volume1.

A link containing the individual code snippets that can be opened in Google Colaboratory are also provided with each piece of code. When you go to the python notebook links provided with each code snippet, you should see an option to open in Colaboratory like the screenshot below.

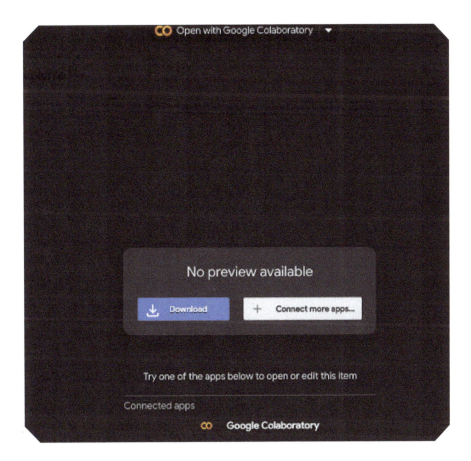

If you do not see this option, you might need to install the Google Colaboratory plugin in your browser.

Python Exercises

1. Accuracy with Binary Classification

What it does
- Calculates the accuracy of two lists (binary case).

    a. Without using libraries

    b. Using libraries

Link to the code in a python notebook: https://bit.ly/33DULRq

Note that the above code can be opened in GoogleColaboratory. To view python code in this notebook, you will need the Google Colaboratory plugin installed in the browser.

CODE

```
[ ] # Change the lists; 'actual_labels' and 'ai_predictions' as you needed

    # Actual labels
    actual_labels = ['cat', 'cat', 'dog', 'cat', 'dog']

    # Predicted labels
    ai_predictions = ['cat', 'dog', 'dog', 'cat', 'cat']

[ ] # Initialise the variable to count the no. of correctly predicted labels
    correct_predictions = 0

    # Iterate through the each index of actual labels in the list 'labels'
    for label in range(len(actual_labels)):

        # Check whether the predicted label is same as the actual label
        if actual_labels[label] == ai_predictions[label]:

            # If predicted label is same as the actual label, increase the correct predictions by 1
            correct_predictions += 1

    # Calculate the accuracy
    accuracy_without_sklearn = correct_predictions / len(actual_labels)

    # Calculate the accuracy percentage
    accuracy_percentage_without_sklearn = accuracy_without_sklearn * 100

    # Print the accuracy
```

```
    # Print the accuracy
    print ('Accuracy without using sklearn: ', accuracy_without_sklearn)

    # Print the percentage of the accuracy
    print ('Accuracy percentage without using sklearn: ', str(accuracy_percentage_without_sklearn), '%')


[ ] # Import accuracy_score function to calculate the accuracy
    from sklearn.metrics import accuracy_score


[ ] # Calculate the accuracy
    accuracy_using_sklearn =  accuracy_score(actual_labels, ai_predictions)

    # Calculate the accuracy percentage
    accuracy_percentage_using_sklearn = accuracy_using_sklearn * 100

    # Print the accuracy
    print ('\nAccuracy using sklearn: ', accuracy_using_sklearn)

    # Print the percentage of the accuracy
    print ('Accuracy percentage using sklearn: ', str(accuracy_percentage_using_sklearn), '%')
```

Python Exercises

2. Accuracy with Multi-Class Classification

What it does
- Calculates the accuracy of two lists (3 category case).

    a. Without using libraries

    b. Using libraries

Link to the code in a python notebook: https://bit.ly/3p7PMzU

Note that the above code can be opened in GoogleColaboratory. To view python code in this notebook, you will need the Google Colaboratory plugin installed in the browser.

CODE

```
[ ]  # Change the lists; 'actual_labels' and 'ai_predictions' as you needed

     # Actual labels
     actual_labels = ['cat', 'cat', 'racoon', 'racoon', 'dog', 'cat', 'dog', 'racoon']

     # Predicted labels
     ai_predictions = ['racoon', 'cat', 'racoon', 'dog', 'dog', 'cat', 'cat', 'dog']

[ ]  # Initialise the variable to count the no. of correctly predicted labels
     correct_predictions = 0

     # Iterate through the each index of actual labels in the list 'labels'
     for label in range(len(actual_labels)):

         # Check whether the predicted label is same as the actual label
         if actual_labels[label] == ai_predictions[label]:

             # If predicted label is same as the actual label, increase the correct predictions by 1
             correct_predictions += 1

     # Calculate the accuracy
     accuracy_without_sklearn = correct_predictions / len(actual_labels)

     # Calculate the accuracy percentage
     accuracy_percentage_without_sklearn = accuracy_without_sklearn * 100

     # Print the accuracy
     print ('Accuracy without using sklearn: ', accuracy_without_sklearn)

     # Print the percentage of the accuracy
```

Python Exercises

```
    # Print the percentage of the accuracy
    print ('Accuracy percentage without using sklearn: ', str(accuracy_percentage_without_sklearn), '%')


[ ]  # Import accuracy_score function to calculate the accuracy
    from sklearn.metrics import accuracy_score

[ ]  # Claculate the accuracy
    accuracy_using_sklearn =  accuracy_score(actual_labels, ai_predictions)

    # Calculate the accuracy percentage
    accuracy_percentage_using_sklearn = accuracy_using_sklearn * 100

    # Print the accuracy
    print ('\nAccuracy using sklearn: ', accuracy_using_sklearn)

    # Print the percentage of the accuracy
    print ('Accuracy percentage using sklearn: ', str(accuracy_percentage_using_sklearn), '%')
```

Python Exercises

3. Confusion Matrix with Binary Classification

What it does
- This Python program takes two lists, list _1 is labels and list_2 is AI predictions that contains 2 categories. Then the confusion matrix is calculated.

Link to the code in a python notebook: https://bit.ly/3Ic71HQ

Note that the above code can be opened in GoogleColaboratory. To view python code in this notebook, you will need the Google Colaboratory plugin installed in the browser.

CODE

```python
[ ]  # Import confusion_matrix for sklearn based calculation
     from sklearn.metrics import confusion_matrix

     # Import pandas for pandas based calculation
     import pandas as pd

[ ]  # Actuals
     actuals = ['cat', 'cat', 'dog', 'cat', 'dog']

     # Predictions
     predictions = ['cat', 'dog', 'dog', 'cat', 'cat']

[ ]  # Construct Confusion Matrix
     constructed_confusion_matrix = confusion_matrix(predictions, actuals)

     # Print Confusion Matrix
     print("Confusion matrix using sklearn \n \n", constructed_confusion_matrix)
```

Python Exercises

```
[ ]  # Convert actual list to a series
     actuals = pd.Series(actuals, name='Actual')

     # Convert prediction list to a series
     predictions = pd.Series(predictions, name='Predictions')

     # Create Confusion Matrix
     confusion_matrix = pd.crosstab(predictions, actuals)

     # Print Confusion Matrix
     print("\n Confusion matrix using pandas \n \n", confusion_matrix)


      Confusion matrix using pandas

      Actual        cat  dog
      Predictions
      cat            2    1
      dog            1    1
```

Python Exercises

4. Confusion Matrix with Multi-Class Classification

What it does
- This Python program takes two lists, list _1 is labels and list_2 is AI predictions that contains 3 categories. Then the confusion matrix is calculated.

Link to the code in a python notebook: https://bit.ly/36pf9GZ

Note that the above code can be opened in GoogleColaboratory. To view python code in this notebook, you will need the Google Colaboratory plugin installed in the browser.

CODE

```
[ ]  # Import confusion_matrix for sklearn based calculation
     from sklearn.metrics import confusion_matrix

     # Import pandas for pandas based calculation
     import pandas as pd

[ ]  # Actuals
     actuals = ['cat', 'cat', 'racoon', 'racoon', 'dog', 'cat', 'dog', 'racoon']

     # Predictions
     predictions = ['racoon', 'cat', 'racoon', 'dog', 'dog', 'cat', 'cat', 'racoon']

[ ]  # Construct Confusion Matrix
     constructed_confusion_matrix = confusion_matrix(predictions, actuals)

     # Print Confusion Matrix
     print("Confusion matrix using sklearn \n \n", constructed_confusion_matrix)

     Confusion matrix using sklearn

     [[2 1 0]
      [0 1 1]
      [1 0 2]]
```

Python Exercises

```python
[ ]  # Convert actual list to a series
     actuals = pd.Series(actuals, name='Actual')

     # Convert prediction list to a series
     predictions = pd.Series(predictions, name='Predictions')

     # Create Confusion Matrix
     confusion_matrix = pd.crosstab(predictions, actuals)

     # Print Confusion Matrix
     print("\n Confusion matrix using pandas \n \n", confusion_matrix)


      Confusion matrix using pandas

      Actual       cat  dog  racoon
      Predictions
      cat           2    1     0
      dog           0    1     1
      racoon        1    0     2
```

Teachers Corner

Core Concepts

Chapter 5 begins Unit 2, where students delve deeper into different types of AIs. Classification is one of the most important and powerful types of AI. After studying this chapter, students should be able to:

- Understand what distinguishes classification from other types of AI
- Understand that any type of data can be used as features for classification (numbers, categories, text, images, video, etc.) It is only the label that decides the problem as classification.
- There are many different AI algorithms for classification.
- Any classification solution can be measured by the metrics of accuracy and confusion matrix.
- Understand what they can learn from a Confusion Matrix that they cannot from Accuracy.
- Appreciate the uses of classification in the real world.

Grade Level Alignment

The concepts in this chapter are accessible to students in any middle school or high school grade. The plugged exercises at the end of the chapter can also be used by students in any middle school or high school grade. The python coding exercises however, are more suitable for students in grades 8 and above, or any student that has familiarity with the following python elements

- Input/Output
- Loops and Conditionals
- Modules
- The Pandas Module and DataFrames
- SciKit Learn Module

The Curriculum section below contains introductions to all of these Python elements.

Tips

The concepts in this chapter can be understood without doing any of the plugged exercises or code exercises, but doing the plugged exercise is strongly recommended.

Teachers Corner

The students do not need any coding knowledge to do the plugged exercise. Encourage students to explore the classification AI they build to get a better understanding of how classification AIs work.

The coding exercises are optional but encouraged for high school students in computer science classes. Doing these exercises will give the students greater appreciation of how AIs are built in code.

Curriculum

Full curriculum covering chapters 1-10 is available at https://aiclub.world/teachers-material-book-volume-1
Curriculum for Unit 2 (Chapters 5-6) is available at https://aiclub.world/teachers-material-introduction-to-machine-learning. Our teacher's curriculum include lesson guides, videos, presentation material, additional exercises, and assessments, as well as online support.

Scan the QR code for Unit 2 curriculum (Chapters 5-6)

Scan the QR code for the teacher curriculum of this book

Assessment Key

Answer key to the assessment questions in the book can be found here: https://aiclub.world/teachers-material-introduction-to-machine-learning

CHAPTER

6

Regression

Artificial Intelligence services that predict numbers, rather than from a fixed set of categories, are called regression. In this chapter, several examples are presented to understand this type of AI.

What is Regression?

Regression is a type of AI where the goal is to predict a numerical value. The number can be a decimal value or an integer value (whole number). The number can also be positive or negative. For example, one might want the AI to predict the price of a house. The price could be any value such as $200,000 or $212, $456.56, etc. Just like classification problems, it does not matter what the input to the AI (the question) was. The input data can be numbers, categories, text, images, any combination of these, or anything else. It is only the format of the answer, the prediction, that determines whether the AI problem is regression.

Figure 6.1 Analyzing data for prediction

Regression is a type of supervised learning since the label value (which is numerical here) has to be known by the AI before it can learn the pattern. Once it learns the pattern, it can map questions to a numerical value as an answer. Figure 6.2 shows an example regression dataset. In this dataset, the AI will learn how to predict the price of a house based on two pieces of information, *square footage* and the *age* of the house.

sq_ft	age	price
895	26	707158
827	61	285327
873	58	365744
847	58	338163
801	66	204300
522	58	14117
784	46	388363
450	25	121220
657	33	381713
425	52	82357

Figure 6.2: An example regression dataset

Regression

The only factor that determines whether an AI is of type classification or regression is the prediction label. If the label is a number, no matter what the input (features), it is a regression problem.

Regression with Numerical and Categorical Data

Figure 6.3 shows an example of regression with numerical and categorical data. In this case, an insurance company is trying to determine the medical charges that a customer might incur. There are two features, *Age* and *Gender*, where *Age* is numerical and *Gender* is categorical. The label column *Charges* has numerical values and hence this is a regression problem.

Age	Gender	Chargers
45	F	423.89
32	M	334.15
58	F	231.1
26	M	451.5

Figure 6.3: Regression with numerical and categorical input features.

Context

Regression in Real Life

Regression is very widely used for many real-world applications. An example is forecasting, where one can predict the future demand of a product based on historical values. Another example is the optimization of business processes such as predicting customer satisfaction in a call center based on wait times. Such data-driven approaches in businesses help with making operations efficient. Another example: setting up automated alerts, where a regression AI can predict an impending breakdown and alert in advance. For example, if a factory is operating a furnace and the AI uses features such as load, temperature and coolant temperature to predict the temperature of the furnace in the next hour, it can be used to create alerts when the temperature is predicted to rise beyond a certain threshold even before the event actually happens.

Regression with Text Data

Figure 6.4 shows an example of regression with text data. In this case the feature is English text (which can be anything from a single character to many sentences) describing the movie and the prediction is a number that rates the movie on a scale between 1 and 5.

Review	Rating
Loved watching the movie, excellent acting!	4.5
Predictable story with average dialogues	2.7
Not a novel story, but a good take on a popular theme	3.6
Enjoyed it in spite of a predictable storyline	4.3

Figure 6.4: Regression with text data

How is Regression Measured?

Supervised learning algorithms are measured by splitting the data into a training set and a validation set. The training set is used to train the AI and create a model. The validation set is used to test the AI using the model created by the training set. Regression, like classification, is a supervised learning method and hence the same process is followed to measure the performance of a regression AI. In this section, the popular metrics used to measure regression are discussed.

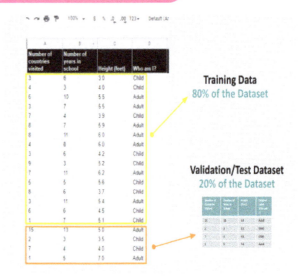

Figure 6.5 Training data and test data

Mean Absolute Error

In Chapter 5, accuracy was described as a metric that measures the overall performance of a classification AI. In the case of classification, it is very clear if the AI is right or wrong about an answer. However, applying the same to a regression problem is tricky. For example, if an AI predicts the temperature for tomorrow and it is quite close, but not exact, how can one measure how good the AI is? One way to do this is to simply measure the error. Error here is the difference between the predicted value and the correct value.

House Prices Prediction

Figure 6.6 House price prediction

Websites like Redfin, Zillow, Realtor, etc. provide estimates of the prices of houses. The algorithm that predicts the house price values is a Regression algorithm. It takes into account features like location, square footage of the house, age of the house, etc. to create these estimates. This provides users of these websites an estimate to compare with the price at which a house is listed in the market.

True Value	Predicted Value	Error	Absolute Error
71	70	1	1
10	11	-1	1
10	9	1	1
11	14	-3	3

Figure 6.7 Measuring the error on each sample

For example, if the temperature that the AI predicted is 70 and the correct value was 71, then the error is 71-70 = 1. Consider another example where the AI predicts 11 and the correct value is 10. Then, the error is 11-10 =1. This implies that the AI is off from the true value by 1. If the AI predicts the exact value, the error is 0.

In another example where the correct value is 10 and the AI predicted 9, the error is -1. The AI is off by 1 in this case too. However, the error value is negative. Does it matter whether the error is positive or negative? From the point of view of creating a metric to measure the average performance of an AI, it does not matter. Therefore, something called an absolute value is calculated. Taking the absolute value of a number means that weather it is a positive number or a negative number does not matter. In this case, for example, the absolute value of -1 is 1. Another example would be the absolute value of -10, which would be 10. The absolute value of 10 is also 10.

The absolute error of an AI indicates that the prediction of the AI was off by the value specified by the error.

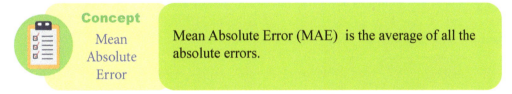

Concept
Mean Absolute Error

Mean Absolute Error (MAE) is the average of all the absolute errors.

Going back to the concept of accuracy, it is calculated by asking the AI multiple questions and then checking how many it got correctly. Similarly, when a regression AI predicts, it provides a set of answers. This results in a set of error values. In the case of accuracy, the number of correct answers is counted. In the case of a set of errors, they need to be combined in such a way that we get a global metric.

For example, if the AI got errors, 1.2, 5.1, 2, 3, etc. The average of all the errors can be calculated to get a single metric describing the average error of the AI. The absolute value for all errors is calculated before averaging them since the direction of the error does not matter. This indicates on average how off the AI is from the right prediction. This popular metric is called Mean Absolute Error (MAE).

In the case of accuracy, the higher the number, the better the AI is. 100% accuracy is the best and zero accuracy is the worst. In contrast, a low value of error indicates a better-performing AI. An average error of 0 implies that the AI makes perfect predictions all the time. Unlike accuracy, which has the worst value of zero, there is no limit to how bad an error can be. MAE can be any value. The higher the MAE, the worse the AI.

Root Mean Square Error

Another popular metric used to measure the performance of a regression AI is RMSE, short for Root Mean Square Error. To calculate this metric, a square of the error values is calculated before taking the average value. A square root of the average value is taken to get the Root of the Mean of the Squared Error values.

Key Insight

In the case of accuracy, the higher the number, the better it is. 100% accuracy is the best you can get and zero accuracy is really bad. In contrast, for regression metrics MAE and RMSE, a low value of error indicates a high-performance AI. Zero error is the best possible error.

Context

Regression in Real Life: Dynamic Pricing

Dynamic pricing is essentially different prices for different situations. This could be different prices for different customers, different prices at different times for the same customer, etc. Broadly adjusting prices to meet various kinds of situations, like increases in demand and changing prices in response to what competitors are doing, is called dynamic pricing. With regression AIs, companies can predict prices for anything.

Dynamic pricing is not unique to AI, it has been going on for a very long time. For example, it has been pretty standard for a long time that air tickets cost more when not booked well in advance. Last-minute tickets for pretty much anything always seem to cost more. Dynamic pricing did not show up because of AI. However, AI made dynamic pricing far more adaptive, and far more responsive to lots of different kinds of situations. After the advent of AI in dynamic pricing, prices can change every minute. For example, they can change based on things that recently occurred in the news.

An item's price might change based on other things the customer recently bought. It could change based on how many other people are looking to buy the same item. One such example is surge pricing in Uber or Lyft. AI is changing the way that products of all kinds, whether they be slots on a freeway or actual physical products, are priced and sold. It also means that, for companies, the more they know about their customers and the more that they know about what's going on in the world that might impact their product, the more they can find the right price for everything at any point in time.

Regression

Characteristics of a Good Regression AI

We have so far seen that 0 is the best MAE or RMSE value that an AI can achieve for a regression problem. However, in the real world, creating a regression AI with 0 error almost never happens. Most AIs will have an RMSE or MAE value that is not zero. Given an RMSE value, how can one decide if it is a good enough AI? For example, if the MAE value is equal to 10, would that be considered a good AI? This depends on what is being predicted.

If the price of a house is being predicted and the AI is off by $10, that is an acceptable MAE value. However, if the AI is predicting the temperature and is off by 10 degrees Centigrade, it is not an acceptable error. The scale of the label being predicted by the AI determines whether a given MAE value is acceptable or not.

A second thing to consider is whether the AI is better than random guessing. In the case of classification and accuracy, a 50% accuracy is the baseline when the AI predicts 2 categories. If the AI predicts 3 categories, 33.33% is the baseline. Similarly, regression also has a baseline. Figure 6.8 is used to learn how to calculate this baseline.

There are 4 samples in this dataset and *Charges* is the prediction variable. To make the best guess of a prediction value without any AI, the best chance at it would be to take an average of the column *Charges*. Average of the column is $(423.89 + 334.15 + 231.1 + 451.5)/4 = 360.16$. This would be the value that is predicted irrespective of the values in *Age* and *Gender*. This is the baseline that the AI has to be better than. If the AI performs worse than this baseline, it is not useful to have an AI at all. The baseline error in this case (MAE) is 77.54.

Age	Gender	Charges
45	F	423.89
32	M	334.15
58	F	231.1
26	M	451.5

Figure 6.8: Sample data

Figure 6.9 shows an example scenario, where the absolute error for the four samples is calculated. Mean Absolute Error is the average of the absolute errors of the samples, which is $(63.73 + 26.01 + 129.06 + 91.34)/4 = 77.535$. In this case, the AI is not good. A good AI is expected to have an MAE much better than the baseline MAE of 77.535.

Charges	Absolute Error
423.89	63.73
334.15	26.01
231.1	129.06
451.5	91.34

Figure 6.9: Prediction and Error

Common Regression Algorithms

There are many AI algorithms that can perform regression. Some are listed below
- Linear Regression (covered later in this book)
- K Nearest Neighbors (covered later in this book)
- Neural Networks (covered later in this book)
- Decision Trees (Covered in Volume 2)

What do these algorithms have in common? They are all able to find patterns in the input data and map it to a numerical value which is the prediction. You can also use the metrics of MAE and RMSE to decide if each algorithm is doing a good job predicting the label in your data. You can compare the different algorithms using these metrics and select the best one.

 Context Demand Forecasting

The process of predicting the demand of products is called demand forecasting. Such forecasting is very important for manufacturers and retailers to manage production processes.

Think about shopping at a store. As a customer, you expect products to be always available. Customers are not happy when something they want to purchase is out of stock. Being able to forecast demand, even across seasonal variations, is very important for businesses to keep their customers happy.

Figure 6.10 Forecasting demand

The concept of demand forecasting has been there for a long time before AI came into the picture. With the advent of AI, the process of forecasting has become more accurate and fine grained. AI also makes it easier to use historical data to forecast demand.

These AI algorithms are not perfect though. Their predictions are based on trends they see in historical data. For example, they cannot adapt to sudden changes in supply or demand that occur due to environmental conditions. For example, sudden heat waves might increase the demand for air conditioning units. The COVID pandemic caused a disruption that the algorithms had no hope of coping with because it was not an event they have been trained for. However, in general, these algorithms have proved to be quite effective for helping businesses manage their supply chains.

Assessment

1. What type of AI is regression? (a) Supervised (b) Unsupervised.

2. List the data type constraints on features for a task to qualify as a regression problem.

3. How is the performance of a regression AI measured?

4. If an AI predicted values [100, 30, 50, 60, 95], while the true values were [98, 32, 51, 55, 88], what is the mean absolute error?

5. What is the difference between MAE and RMSE?

6. Fill in the blanks

(a) Regression is a type of AI where the AI predicts a _____.

(b) Difference between what the AI predicts and the true value is called _____ in regression.

(c) The lowest possible MAE a regression AI can have is _____

7. List a few AI algorithms that can be used for a regression task.

8. Calculate the MAE and RMSE for the below table

Text	Rating	Prediction
loved the food	4.2	4.8
long wait, hated the service	1.2	2
delicious chips!	4.5	4.6
yummy fast food	4.8	4.8

Online Activities

1. Regression AI to Predict House Prices

In this activity, we will do a simple exercise to predict house prices in any given neighborhood by downloading the latest public data available. Please go to https://aiclub.world/activity-house-prices to start this activity!

In this activity, we will learn
• Data collection to build an AI
• Building an AI to solve a Regression problem
• Evaluating the performance of a regression problem

This activity has an interactive component where students will enter different values for features such as the number of bedrooms and square footage of a house and the AI will predict the price of the house.

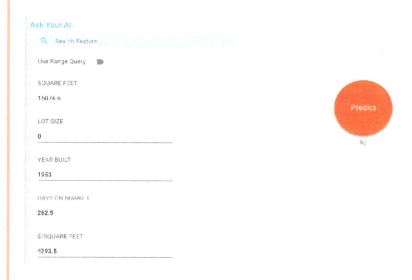

To do the interactive activity, you will need a computer with a chrome browser.

Python Exercises

Python code is provided in this module to help students get hands-on experience interacting with concepts covered in the chapter. The code snippets are kept simple and self-contained. All the code included in this book is available in a GitHub repository https://github.com/pyxeda/MiddleSchoolCurriculum/tree/master/Volume1.

A link containing the individual code snippets that can be opened in Google Colaboratory are also provided with each piece of code. When you go to the python notebook links provided with each code snippet, you should see an option to open in Colaboratory like the screenshot below.

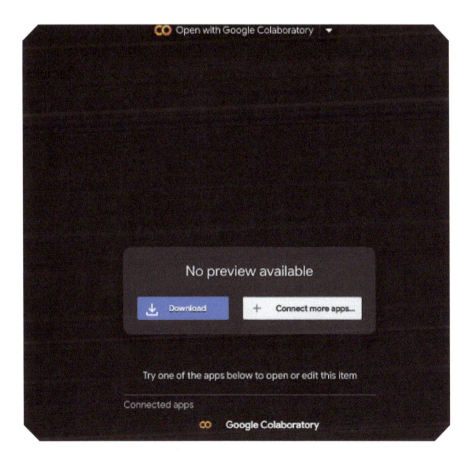

If you do not see this option, you might need to install the Google Colaboratory plugin in your browser.

Python Exercises

1. Mean Absolute Error

What it does

- Calculates the mean absolute error between two lists, AI predictions and the labels.

Link to the code in a python notebook: https://bit.ly/36pf9GZ

Note that the above code can be opened in GoogleColaboratory. To view python code in this notebook, you will need the Google Colaboratory plugin installed in the browser.

CODE

```
[ ]  # Import mean_absolute_error for sklearn based calculation
     from sklearn.metrics import mean_absolute_error


[ ]  # Actuals
     actuals = [12, 13, 14, 15, 15, 22, 27]

     # Predictions
     predictions = [11, 13, 14, 14, 15, 55, 35]
```

```
[ ]    # Variable to count the no. of actual items
       count = 0

       # Variable to get absolute error sum
       absolute_error_sum = 0

       # Iterate through each item of the list 'actuals'
       for item in range(len(actuals)):

           # Increase the count by 1, when iterating
           count += 1

           # Calculate the difference between actual value and predicted value
           error = actuals[item] - predictions[item]

           # Get absolute value of the error using 'abs' function
           absolute_error = abs(error)

           # Sum up the errors
           absolute_error_sum += absolute_error

       # Calculate the mean absolute error
       mae_without_sklearn = absolute_error_sum / count

       # Print the MAE value
       print ('Mean Absolute Error without sklearn : ', mae_without_sklearn)

       Mean Absolute Error without sklearn :   6.142857142857143


[ ]    # Calculate MAE using sklearn
       mae_with_sklearn = mean_absolute_error(actuals, predictions)

       # Print the MAE value
       print ('Mean Absolute Error with sklearn : ', mae_with_sklearn)

       Mean Absolute Error with sklearn :   6.142857142857143
```

Python Exercises

2. Root Mean Square Error

What it does
- Calculates the root mean square error between two lists, AI predictions and the labels.

Link to the code in a python notebook: https://bit.ly/3h2WhzF
Note that the above code can be opened in GoogleColaboratory. To view python code in this notebook, you will need the Google Colaboratory plugin installed in the browser.

CODE

```
[ ]  # Change the lists; 'actual_labels' and 'ai_predictions' as you needed

     # Actual labels
     actual_labels = [1, 2, 5, 2.3, 5, 4.6, 3.7]

     # Predicted labels
     ai_predictions = [-1, 4, 3, 4.3, 7, 2.6, 5]

[ ]  # Initialise the variable to sum up all the squared errors
     squaredErrorSum = 0

     # Iterate through the each index of actual labels in the list 'labels'
     for label in range(len(actual_labels)):

         # Calculate the error between actual label and predicted label
         error = actual_labels[label] - ai_predictions[label]

         # Square the error found in above step
         squareError = error**2

         # Sum up the squared errors
         squaredErrorSum += squareError

     # Calculate the mean square error
     mse_without_sklearn = squaredErrorSum / len(actual_labels)
```

Regression

Python Exercises

```
    # Calculate the root mean square error
    rmse_without_sklearn = mse_without_sklearn ** 0.5

    # Print the rmse value
    print ('RMSE without using sklearn: ', rmse_without_sklearn)

    RMSE without using sklearn:  1.9157244060668015
```

```
[ ]  # Import mean_squared_error function for error calculations
     from sklearn.metrics import mean_squared_error

     # Import sqrt function to get the square root of the mean_squared_error
     from math import sqrt
```

```
[ ]  # Calculate the mean squared error
     mse_using_sklearn = mean_squared_error(actual_labels, ai_predictions)

     # Calculate the root mean squared error
     rmse_using_sklearn = sqrt(mse_using_sklearn)

     # Print the rmse value
     print ('RMSE using sklearn: ', rmse_using_sklearn)

     RMSE using sklearn:  1.9157244060668015
```

Teachers Corner

Core Concepts

Chapter 6 introduced Regression, another very important and powerful type of AI that is used everyday in industries from marketing to sales to finance. After studying this chapter, students should be able to:

- Understand the difference between Classification and regression
- Appreciate that, like Classification, Regression can also be used with any type of feature data (text, numbers, categories, images, etc.) It is only the type of label (numerical) that makes an AI problem a Regression problem.
- Understand why Classification metrics like Accuracy and Confusion Matrix cannot be used to measure Regression.
- Appreciate the use or Error based metrics for regression. Understand the difference between Error based metrics and classification metrics.
- Understand some examples of Regression use around the world.

Grade Level Alignment

The concepts in this chapter are accessible to students in any Middle School or High School grade, with one exception. RMSE is challenging for 6th and 7th grade students and is recommended for students in 8th grade and above.

The plugged exercises at the end of the chapter can also be used by students in any middle school or high school grade. The python coding exercises however, are more suitable for students in grades 8 and above, or any student that has familiarity with the following python elements

- Input/Output
- Loops and Conditionals
- Lists
- Modules
- SciKit Learn Module

The Curriculum section below contains introductions to all of these Python elements.

Tips

The concepts in this chapter can be understood without doing any of the plugged exercises or code exercises, but doing the plugged exercise is strongly recommended.

Teachers Corner

The students do not need any coding knowledge to do the plugged exercise. Encourage students to explore the regression AI they build to get a better understanding of how regression works. Comparing the regression AI they build here to the classification AI they built as part of Plugged Exercises in Chapter 5 will also generate more insight.

Now that students have an understanding of both classification and regression, encourage them to think about whether a regression problem can be made into a classification problem. For example - if the AI is predicting rainfall in inches, that is a regression problem. However, if the label values are made into buckets (for example, any rainfall between 0 and 2 inches is "Low", any between 2 and 5 inches is "Medium", etc.), the same problem can be converted into classification.

The coding exercises are optional but encouraged for high school students in computer science classes. Doing these exercises will give the students greater appreciation of how AIs are built in code.

Curriculum

Full curriculum covering chapters 1-10 is available at https://aiclub.world/teachers-material-book-volume-1
Curriculum for Unit 2 (Chapters 5-6) is available at https://aiclub.world/teachers-material-introduction-to-machine-learning. Our teacher's curriculum include lesson guides, videos, presentation material, additional exercises, and assessments, as well as online support.

Scan the QR code for Unit 2 curriculum (Chapters 5-6)

Scan the QR code for the teacher curriculum of this book

Assessment Key
Answer key to the assessment questions in the book can be found here:
https://aiclub.world/teachers-material-introduction-to-machine-learning

K Nearest Neighbors

In this chapter, a very popular algorithm called KNN is explored. KNN is short for K Nearest Neighbors. This algorithm is quite popular and very easy to understand.

KNN algorithm can be used for both classification and regression types of problems. KNN is used in supervised learning which means the training data for the algorithm contains both features and labels. KNN can predict both, numbers and categories.

Features of the dataset can be anything like numbers, categories, text, etc. In the real world examples, datasets have hundreds of features. Two examples, one for classification and one for regression are presented in this chapter to understand how K Nearest Neighbors works.

How Does a KNN Predict?

KNN can predict both, numbers and categories. The first example shown in Figure 7.1 is one where KNN predicts categories.

In this dataset shown in Figure 7.1, there are only two features, Years in school and height. The label value has two categories, adult or child. We will plot this dataset in two dimensions where the two feature values of the dataset will be on the two axes. It is easy to visualize distance in two dimensions. Using a dataset with only two features helps visualize how a KNN algorithm works.

Years in school	height	label
0	2.18	child
7	5.58	adult
4	5.95	adult
4	4.36	child
2	5.53	adult
9	5.38	child
11	5.29	adult
4	5.91	adult
0	3.96	child
1	2.72	child

Figure 7.1 Example dataset with two features and a label

A plot of the dataset is shown in Figure 7.2. Each row in the table shown in Figure 7.1 is represented by a single dot in the plot in Figure 7.2. The two label categories, child and adult are represented by two colors green and red respectively. All the red points in the plot are adults, and all the green points are children. A visual inspection of the pattern of points in the plot shows that if the height is a small number, then most likely it is a child. If *Years in school* is a large number, then it is most likely an adult, even if the height is a small number. This is the kind of visual insight that plotting the data can provide.

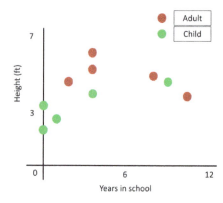

Figure 7.2 Plot of the dataset with features *Years in school* on the x-axis and label *height* on the y-axis

The way a K Nearest Neighbors algorithm makes predictions is easy to understand using a plot. KNN algorithm looks at the training data provided and memorizes it during the training process. It uses the information to figure out the nearest neighbors in the training dataset to any given point. It uses this information to make future predictions. For example, if the KNN algorithm has to make a prediction on whether someone is an adult or a child, like the new point shown in Figure 7.3, it looks at this point in the context of the training data around it.

The new point shown in the Figure 7.3 has *Years in school* around six and height around five. This point is not colored as it is a test point and its membership to either of the categories, adult or child is not known yet. The goal of the KNN algorithm here is to predict this category.

A KNN algorithm that has memorized the training data will look for K Nearest Neighbors to the point. If K is assumed to be one, KNN will look at one nearest point as shown in Figure 7.4.

Since a red point, which represents an adult is the closest neighbor, KNN will predict the new point to be an adult. This is how KNN makes predictions. However, the value of K here can be chosen by the user.

If K is three instead of one, the KNN algorithm looks at three neighbors. Figure 7.5 shows the three closest neighbors. In this case, note that two neighbors are green and one neighbor is red. The algorithm picks green, which is a child as its prediction. This shows that in a K Nearest Neighbors algorithm, depending on the value of K chosen by the user, prediction can be an adult or a child.

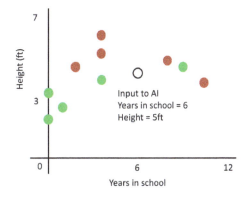

Figure 7.3 A new point shown by the uncolored circle in the plot to illustrate how KNN makes predictions

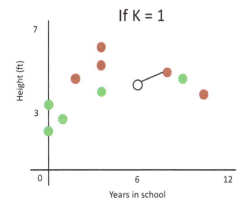

Figure 7.4 Predictions using a KNN model for a value of K=1.

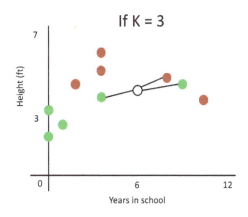

Figure 7.5 Predictions using a KNN model for a value of K=3.

Figure 7.6 shows an example of a regression data set. A data set is regression, when the prediction variable is a continuous number. In this case, price of a house is a continuous number and not a category. The value of the price of a house could be any number and hence it is a regression problem.

Plotting a regression dataset cannot be done using the color-coded approach we followed for the classification case, where each category of the label value was represented using a different color. It is different from classification, where each category can be color-coded. In regression, there are no categories. Using different colors for each unique value will be too many colors and can be visually confusing. A good way to plot for a case like this is to assign every point a number. There is no color-coding, but every point/row has a unique number assigned to it. This number is shown in the column *index* in Figure 7.6. This table is much bigger than the previous one because there is a new column called an index, which is here simply to identify the sample. *Index* is not a feature. The features are the square footage of the house represented by the column *sq_ft* and the *age* of the house. The AI should predict the label which is the *price* of the house.

There are 10 points, and every point represents a single sample plotted in Figure 7.7. KNN follows exactly the same principle that it followed in classification. For example, if a new house comes in, which is around 600 square feet and 28 years old, how does a KNN algorithm predict this value? If the value of K is three, it is going to look at the three nearest neighbors. Here, it turns out that the samples with index seven, eight, and nine are the nearest neighbors.

In this case, what should the price of this house be?

index	sq_ft	age	price
1	895	26	707158
2	827	61	285327
3	873	58	365744
4	847	58	338163
5	801	66	204300
6	522	58	14117
7	784	46	388363
8	450	25	121220
9	657	33	381713
10	425	52	82357

Figure 7.6 Example regression dataset with two features sq_ft, age and a label price.

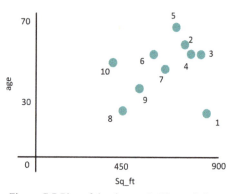

Figure 7.7 Plot of the dataset in Figure 7.6

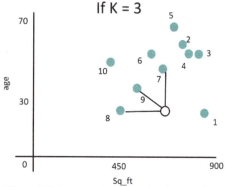

Figure 7.8 A new point shown by the uncolored circle in the plot to illustrate how KNN makes predictions

In the real world, there are several different ways to do this. A straight forward approach is to take the average. Average of the seventh house, the eighth house and the ninth house would be the price of the new house. These are the ways that an AI predicts in the case of KNN for classification, and regression.

Hyper-parameters of KNN

K is a hyper-parameter of KNN. The reason it is called a hyper-parameter is because this value is set by the user and has an impact on how the algorithm behaves. An important question is how do you find the best K? The process of finding the best K is called hyper parameter tuning. It is very hard to give a single value of K as an answer. Every dataset is unique and part of the puzzle is to find out by simply trying out different values. It is something to experiment and find out. Whichever value gives the best performance is the best K for the dataset. The process of figuring out this value of K is called hyper parameter tuning.

In summary, KNN is a very simple algorithm and is very easy to understand. It has a single hype-parameter called K that can be tuned. There are many algorithms that are more sophisticated and have many hyper parameters to tune. In such a case, hyper-parameter tuning can be very complex. KNN has the advantage of being really simple, easy to understand, and easy to hyper parameter tune.

Pitfalls of KNN

Context

Exercise: Guess the House Price

House one is 1000 square feet and zero years old, house two is 800 square feet eight and zero years old. House three is 1000 square feet and 100 years old. The label value is the price of the house. House number two is $10,000 and house number three is $5,000. As a human, if you were to predict the price of house one and you have only two options to pick from, either $10,000 or $5,000, what would you pick?

Square feet	age	Price
1000	0	
800	0	10,000$
1000	100	5,000$

Figure 7.9 A table with two features: Square feet and age, one label Price and just 2 samples in training data.

Let's look at what KNN would pick. If K is equal to one, what is the closest neighbor in terms of the features, which is square footage and age here? It turns out that the distance between house one and house two is 200. The distance between house one and house three is only 100. So, it would pick house 3, whose price is 5000$.

Table in Figure 7.9 is an illustration of one of the pitfalls of KNN. A house which is 100 years old is actually pretty cheap compared to a house that is brand new. The age of a house is much more important than the square footage.

However, KNN completely misses this. KNN does not know that square footage is more important or less important than age, it rates all features equally. However, square footage can be anywhere from 800 to 3000, but age can only be between 0 to 200. People usually do not live in a 1000-year-old house. Typically, houses are between 0 and 200 years old. Clearly, the scale is different. The numbers start differently. Square footage does not start at zero, but age starts at zero. So, the starting point of these features is also different. In addition, the range is also different. This is a drawback of KNN to keep in mind. If an awesome data set that is supposed to do really well with the AI, is giving bad predictions, then think about whether the features in the dataset have different scales.

There are a lot of approaches that researchers have come up with to make sure that one can indirectly tell KNN that one feature is more important than the other. For the specific example in Figure 7.9, one really easy way to do this is, multiply all values of age with 1000. Then the value of age is between zero and 200,000 instead of being between 0 and 200. Such multiplication with a constant number artificially increases the range of age. Alternatively, one can divide all the values of square feet by a constant number to make sure that they are more or less equal in range. This process of modifying the dataset by multiplying or dividing the column values with a fixed number is called feature engineering. How do you decide what would be a good number to multiply or divide the columns with? A straightforward approach would be to try out several different values and measure the KNN performance in each case. The value that yields the best performance can be the value that is picked for the feature engineering of the dataset. This is one example of how the drawback of KNN can be overcome.

Another important pitfall of KNN to keep in mind is that it can only predict a value that is in the range of training data. If for example, KNN needs to predict the price of a house whose square footage is much larger than the maximum value present in training data, KNN can only refer to the closest examples in training data. It will not be able to scale up the price of the house proportionally.

Assessment

1. What types of problems can KNN make predictions for? (a) Regression only (b) Classification only (c) Classification and Regression (d) None

2. What does the K in the KNN algorithm represent?

3. How would a KNN algorithm behave when the value of K is equal to the number of samples in the training dataset?

4. If a training dataset has three features, *volume*, *weight* and *viscosity* and the label *density*, what can you do to make the algorithm give more importance to the feature *volume* than others, when it makes predictions?

5. KNN is a type of unsupervised algorithm (a) True (b) False.

6. Fill in the blanks

(a) KNN algorithm predictions may change when you vary the value of _____.

(b) KNN is short for _____.

(c) Hyper-parameter of the KNN algorithm is called _____.

7. A KNN algorithm can only have two features in the dataset (a) True (b) False

8. A training dataset for regression has labels in the range 100 and 200. Can a KNN algorithm predict a label value of 300 for any combination of feature values?

9. I have a dataset, where the label is *yes* or *no* based on three features, all of which are numerical. Can a KNN model be used here to make predictions? Please explain.

10. What are some drawbacks of a KNN algorithm?

Online Activities

1. Create a KNN Model

In this activity, one can train a K-nearest neighbors model on a large dataset. Please go to the link https://aiclub.world/knn

One can use the pre-loaded datasets or bring in your own. Train a KNN model and see how well it does. You can view the model performance metrics such as accuracy and confusion matrix and optimize it for different values of K.

The advantage of this activity is that it caters to very large datasets.

Unplugged Activities

1. K Nearest Neighbors on Paper

In this activity, students will make predictions like KNN by creating their own unique dataset.

Materials Needed:
Paper
Color pens
String
Push pins

Description:
Step 1: Students should put dots on a paper with 2 different colors
Step 2: Put a push pin at a random location on the paper
Step 3: Select an odd value of K from the set (1,3,5)
Step 4: Use the string to find the K nearest dots
Step 5: Note the color of the dots
Step 6: The push pin is classified as the color of majority of these dots

2. Find the Best K Value:
Figure 7.10 shows the plot of a training dataset for KNN. Yellow and Green colors represent two categories: Banana and Apple. Find the prediction of KNN for the table given in Figure 7.11, by trying different values of K.

Find the value of K with best accuracy

Weight	Length	Prediction	Label
4	4		Apple
3.5	5.5		Banana
3.2	5		Apple
4.2	7		Banana

Figure 7.11 Example dataset

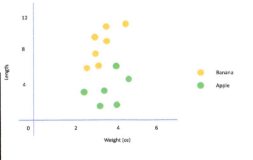

Figure 7.10 Plot of data in Figure 7.11

Python Exercises

Python code is provided in this module to help students get hands-on experience interacting with concepts covered in the chapter. The code snippets are kept simple and self-contained. All the code included in this book is available in a GitHub repository https://github.com/pyxeda/MiddleSchoolCurriculum/tree/master/Volume1.

A link containing the individual code snippets that can be opened in Google Colaboratory are also provided with each piece of code. When you go to the python notebook links provided with each code snippet, you should see an option to open in Colaboratory like the screenshot below.

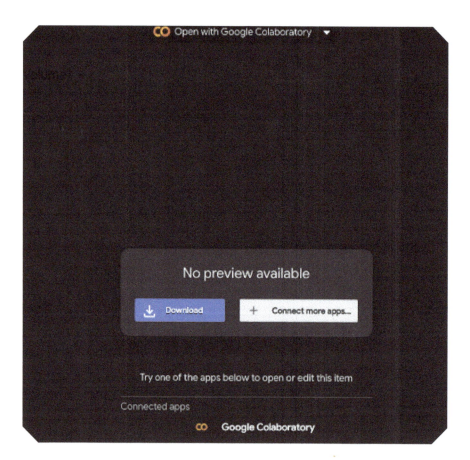

If you do not see this option, you might need to install the Google Colaboratory plugin in your browser.

Python Exercises

1. K-Nearest Neighbors Classification

What it does
- This code reads a csv file, trains a knn classification model on the dataset and then calculates the accuracy and confusion matrix.

Link to the code in a python notebook: https://bit.ly/3JEpGfG

Note that the above code can be opened in GoogleColaboratory. To view python code in this notebook, you will need the Google Colaboratory plugin installed in the browser.

CODE

```
[ ]  # Import pandas module to read the CSV file and to process the tabular data
     import pandas as pd

     # Import train_test_split to split data as test and train
     from sklearn.model_selection import train_test_split

     # Import KNeighborsClassifier class to get the KNN object
     from sklearn.neighbors import KNeighborsClassifier

     # Import accuracy_score and confusion_matrix functions for accuracy calculations
     from sklearn.metrics import accuracy_score, confusion_matrix

     # Import gdown module to download files from google drive
     import gdown


[ ]  # Please change the url as needed (make sure you have the access to the file)
     url = "https://drive.google.com/file/d/1J5z80sAtgSp9i1eLxQFoxVexSZJuhI_-/view?usp=sharing"

     # Derive the file id from the url
     file_id = url.split('/')[-2]

     # Derive the download url of the file
     download_url = 'https://drive.google.com/uc?id=' + file_id
```

```
    # Give the file name you want to save it
    file_name = "child_vs_adult.csv"

    # Derive the file location
    file_location = "/content/" + file_name

[ ] # Download the file from drive
    gdown.download(download_url, file_location, quiet=False)

    # Read the CSV file
    data = pd.read_csv(file_location)


[ ] # Print a sample from the csv dataset
    print('---------- First 5 rows of the Dataset ----------\n', data.head())


[ ] # Please change the target variable according to the dataset
    # You can refer to the dataset details printed in the above step
    target_column = 'who_am_I'

    # Seperate the training data by removing the target column
    X = data.drop(columns=[target_column])

    # Separate the target values
    y = data[target_column].values

    # Split the dataset into train and test data
    X_train, X_test, y_train, y_test = train_test_split(X, y, test_size=0.2, random_state=1, stratify=y)

    # Create KNN classifier
    # You can change the n_neighbors in order to get a higher accuracy
    knn = KNeighborsClassifier(n_neighbors = 20)

    # Train the model
    knn.fit(X_train, y_train)

    # Predict using test values
    y_pred = knn.predict(X_test)

    # Get actual values and predicted values into a table
    predicted_results = pd.DataFrame({'Actual': y_test, 'Predicted': y_pred})
    print('---------- Predicted Results ----------\n', predicted_results)
```

K Nearest Neighbors

Python Exercises

```
[ ]   # Calculate the confusion matrix
      confusion_mat = confusion_matrix(y_test, y_pred)
      print ('---------- Confusion Matrix of Your Model ----------\n', confusion_mat)


[ ]   # Calculate accuracy using 'accuracy_score'
      accuracy = accuracy_score(y_test, y_pred)
      print('---------- Accuracy of Your Model ----------\n', accuracy)
```

Python Exercises

2. K-Nearest Neighbors Regression

What it does
- This code reads a csv file, trains a knn regression model on the dataset and then calculates the MAE and RMSE metrics.

Link to the code in a python notebook: https://bit.ly/3IbZJDU

Note that the above code can be opened in GoogleColaboratory. To view python code in this notebook, you will need the Google Colaboratory plugin installed in the browser.

CODE

```
[ ]  # Import pandas module to read the CSV file and to process the tabular data
     import pandas as pd

     # Import train_test_split to split data as test and train
     from sklearn.model_selection import train_test_split

     # Import KNeighborsRegressor class to get the KNN object
     from sklearn.neighbors import KNeighborsRegressor

     # Import mean_absolute_error and mean_squared_error functions for error calculations
     from sklearn.metrics import mean_absolute_error, mean_squared_error

     # Import sqrt function to get the square root of the mean_squared_error
     from math import sqrt

     # Import gdown module to download files from google drive
     import gdown

[ ]  # Please change the url as needed (make sure you have the access to the file)
     url = 'https://drive.google.com/file/d/1Hxksp6KSjoex0wdER032QypLUYmdLNeg/view?usp=sharing'

     # Derive the file id from the url
     file_id = url.split('/')[-2]

     # Derive the download url of the file
     download_url = 'https://drive.google.com/uc?id=' + file_id

     # Give the file name you want to save it
     file_name = 'average.csv'

     # Derive the file location
     file_location = '/content/' + file_name
```

Python Exercises

```
[ ]  # Download the file from drive
     gdown.download(download_url, file_location, quiet=False)

     # Read the CSV file
     data = pd.read_csv(file_location)


[ ]  # Print a sample from the csv dataset
     print('---------- First 5 rows of the Dataset ----------\n', data.head())

[ ]  # Please change the target variable according to the dataset
     # You can refer to the dataset details printed in the above step
     target_column = 'AVERAGE'

     # Seperate the training data by removing the target column
     X = data.drop(columns=[target_column])

     # Separate the target values
     y = data[target_column].values

     # Split the dataset into train and test data
     X_train, X_test, y_train, y_test = train_test_split(X, y, test_size=0.2)

     # Create KNN regressor
     # You can change the n_neighbors in order to reduce the error
     knn = KNeighborsRegressor(n_neighbors=7)

     # Train the model
     knn.fit(X_train, y_train)

     # Predict using test values
     y_pred = knn.predict(X_test)

     # Get actual values and predicted values into a table
     predicted_results = pd.DataFrame({'Actual': y_test, 'Predicted': y_pred})
     print('---------- Predicted Results ----------\n', predicted_results)

[ ]  # Calculate the MAE
     MAE = mean_absolute_error(y_test, y_pred)
     print ('\nMean Absolute Error (MAE): ', MAE)

[ ]  # Calculate the RMSE
     RMSE = sqrt(mean_squared_error(y_test, y_pred))
     print ('\nRoot Mean Squared Error (RMSE): ', RMSE)
```

Python Exercises

```
[ ]  # Calculate accuracy using 'accuracy_score'
     accuracy = accuracy_score(y_test, y_pred)
     print('---------- Accuracy of Your Model ----------\n', accuracy)
```

Teachers Corner

Core Concepts

K Nearest Neighbors is a simple and powerful algorithm that can be used for both Classification and Regression. Like most AI algorithms, it is not universally useful but is appropriate for specific situations. After studying this chapter, students should be able to:

- Understand how KNN works
- Understand how KNN works a bit differently for Classification and Regression
- Appreciate the strengths and weaknesses of the algorithm
- Identify real-world applications that benefit from KNN
- Understand why K is a key hyper-parameter (tuning knob) for KNN. Appreciate why different values of K can result in different behavior by the same AI algorithm.

Grade Level Alignment

KNN is accessible to students in any middle school or high school grade. Students in grades 8 and above, who have had a course in Algebra, will be able to appreciate in more depth the concept of distance that KNN relies upon.

The plugged exercises are accessible to any student in middle school or high school, who can use them to build an AI with KNN, tune it, and explore how it works. The python coding exercises however, are more suitable for students in grades 8 and above, or any student that has familiarity with the following python elements

- Input/Output
- Loops and Conditionals
- Lists
- Modules
- Pandas and Dataframes
- SciKit Learn Module

The Curriculum section below contains introductions to all of these Python elements.

Teachers Corner

Tips

Encourage students to build the AI in the plugged exercise and tune K themselves. This will help them appreciate that the value of K can change the algorithm's effectiveness very quickly.

If this is done in a class, encourage all the students to tune K and compare what values gave them the best results. They will likely find that the best values of K may not be the same for all of them. This is because there are often many good values of K, sometimes quite far apart. This is normal behavior for AI algorithms, and a good area for students to explore and appreciate.

Curriculum

Full curriculum covering chapters 1-10 is available at https://aiclub.world/teachers-material-book-volume-1
Curriculum for Unit 3 (Chapters 7-10) is available at https://aiclub.world/teachers-material-introduction-to-ai-algorithms. Our teacher's curriculums include lesson guides, videos, presentation material, additional exercises, and assessments, as well as online support.

Scan the QR code for the Unit 3 curriculum (Chapters 7-10)

Scan the QR code for the teacher curriculum of this book

Teachers Corner

Assessment Key

Answer key to the assessment questions in the book can be found here:
https://aiclub.world/teachers-material-introduction-to-ai-algorithms

8

Linear Regression

Linear Regression is a very popular algorithm used for solving the regression type of AI problems. Linear here means that the relationship between features and label is expected to be linear. This chapter covers Linear Regression, how it works, and what types of problems it is suitable for.

Datasets for Linear Regression

Linear regression is a type of supervised learning, which means that the training data for the algorithm contains both features and labels. Linear regression does not predict categories, which means it cannot learn classification types of problems. It is used only for regression, or in other words, problems where the prediction label is a number. Features on the other hand can be anything like numbers, categories, text, etc. In real world uses of linear regression, datasets can have hundreds of features of any of these types or combinations.

To begin, lets explore some examples to understand how linear regression works.

How Does Linear Regression Work?

Linear regression is explored in this section using an example dataset as shown in Figure 8.1.

This is a very simplified dataset for illustration purposes. The first column is the feature and the second column is the label. The AI gets one feature to learn from and it is supposed to predict the label value.

Features	Label
0.2	2.8
0.5	3.6
0.7	4.5
1.0	5.5

Figure 8.1 Example dataset with one feature and label

The plot shown in Figure 8.2 visualizes this data. The x-axis is the feature, and the y-axis is the label. The four green dots correspond to each row of Figure 8.1. For example, the first dot corresponds to the first row. The feature value is 0.2, and the corresponding label is 2.8.

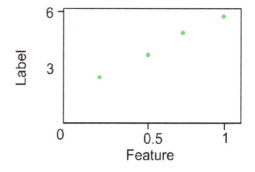

By just looking at this visualization of the data, one can guess the general trend of the data. It follows the pattern of a line. There is a linear relationship between the feature on the x-axis and the label on the y-axis. In addition, a larger value of the feature seems to positively correlate with a larger value of the label value. In other words, as the feature value increases, so does the label.

Figure 8.2 Plot of the dataset with the feature on the x-axis and the label on the y-axis

The red line in Figure 8.3 captures the relationship between the feature and the label. If this is assumed to be the linear regression model, the next step would be to understand how such a model could be used to make predictions. For example, if a new feature has a value of 0.8, how would the linear regression model make a prediction? Table in Figure 8.1 does not have this value as a part of training data.

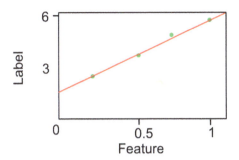

Figure 8.3 A line representing the trend of data in the plot

In order to make predictions using a model represented by the red line, project a line from the value 0.8 on the x-axis to the red line. Then, project a line to the y-axis from the point of intersection at the red line. Figure 8.4 illustrates this using the blue lines. It shows that for an incoming feature value of 0.8, the model would predict 5 as the label. Whether this is an accurate prediction or not depends on how well the red line captures the trend in the data. This would be how predictions are made when the linear regression model is trained on a dataset. Linear regression is often called "line-fitting" for this reason.

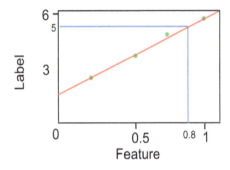

Figure 8.4 Predictions using a linear regression model for an example feature value of 0.8.

Parameters of Linear Regression

The linear regression model is a line that best fits the data. When there is a single feature, it can be visualized as a line but the same idea applies no matter how many features there are. For a single feature, mathematically, this line is represented by the equation (Equation 8.1):

$$Label = w_0 + w_1 \times feature \qquad \text{Equation 8.1}$$

w_0 here is very popularly called the intercept. An intercept is not multiplied with anything. It is a freestanding value. It can potentially take any numerical value.

The second parameter in the above equation is w_1, which is multiplied with the feature. Since there is a single feature, there is only one parameter w_1. This is the equation of the red line in Figure 8.3. Parameters of linear regression are also known as model coefficients.

Going back to the question we answered before, if the incoming feature is 0.8, how would the model predict the label value? Given that the model is a line shown in the equation, the label value will be predicted by substituting the value 0.8 into the equation. This is shown below (Equation 8.2).

$$Label = w_0 + w_1 \times 0.8$$ Equation 8.2

Depending on what the values of w_0 and w_1 are, the label value will be calculated. Therefore, the key during the training process is to determine good values for w_0 and w_1 based on the training data. It is important to understand the impact of the value of w_0 and w_1 on the position and orientation of the line. Different values of w_0 and w_1 will result in different positions and orientations of the line. This is shown in Figure 8.5. Here the feature is x and the prediction/label is y.

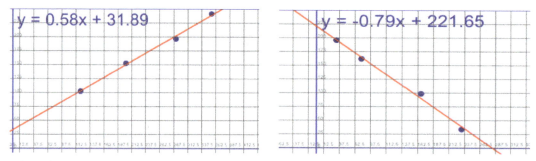

Figure 8.5 Lines with different orientations for different w_0,w_1 values (31.89, 0.58) and (221.65, -0.79)

Similar to the previous example, if we want to find out what the prediction would be for a x value of 0.8, we would simply substitute this value in the line equation. This would be 0.58x0.8 + 31.89 = 32.35 in the first plot and -0.79x0.8+221.65 = 221.02 in the second plot.

Another example dataset is shown in Figure 8.6. The goal here is to predict the price of a house. Here as well, there is a single feature, which is square feet, and the label is the price.

Feature	Label
Square Feet	Price (k$)
1250	500
3200	2200
950	350
2100	950

Figure 8.6 Example dataset with one feature Square Feet and Label Price

A plot visualizing this data is shown in Figure 8.7. The feature, square feet is on the x-axis and the label, the price, is on the y-axis. The price is what the model needs to learn to predict.

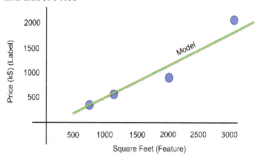

The linear regression equation for this would be (Equation 8.3)

$$Price = w_0 + w_1 \times Square\ Feet$$

Figure 8.7 Plot of data in Figure 8.6

Equation 8.3

Linear Regression

If something else was being predicted, the price would be replaced by whatever needed to be predicted and square feet would be replaced by the feature. Note that this equation remains the same. The way linear regression tries to predict is by fitting a line to your data, and the equation of the line remains the same. The features, label and the model parameters w_0 and w_1 will have different values depending on the problem, but the structure of the equation does not change. This is both the strength and weakness of linear regression. If the line fits the data well, linear regression works great. If the line is not a good fit, linear regression will not work well.

What Happens During Training

During training, a dataset such as the one shown in Figure 8.6 is provided to the algorithm. The linear regression model is represented by (w_0, w_1). These values are unknown and during the training phase, the algorithm figures out the best values for w_0 and w_1. The equation of the linear regression model is given by Equation 8.3. How can an algorithm figure out the perfect values of w_0 and w_1 that would satisfy the following set of equations representing the training dataset?

$$500 = w_0 + w_1 \times 1250$$
$$2200 = w_0 + w_1 \times 3200$$
$$350 = w_0 + w_1 \times 950$$
$$950 = w_0 + w_1 \times 2100$$

Equation 8.4

Mathematically, there are several ways to find values of w_0 and w_1 that satisfy the above conditions. However, in the real world, it is possible that no values of w_0 and w_1 can satisfy all the samples in the training dataset. In such a case, the algorithm figures out the values of (w_0, w_1) that best approximate the above equations for all the training examples on an average. The process of figuring out the best values of (w_0, w_1) based on the training data is called training in linear regression.

Concept

Model Parameters

Model parameters are the values in the model that affect how it converts input data into a prediction. All algorithms generate models and all models have model parameters, but the type of parameters depends on the algorithm. In linear regression, the coefficients of the equation are the model parameters.

It is easy to visualize the line in two dimensions. In three dimensions, this becomes a plane, shown in Figure 8.8.

In higher dimensions, the equation remains the same, but it is hard to visualize it. In higher dimensions, it is called a hyper-plane.

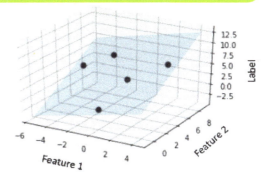

Figure 8.8 A plane in 3D representing the linear regression equation when there are two features

Figure 8.9 shows a dataset with four features. In this case the equation of the linear regression model would have more parameters. Equation 8.5 shows the equation linear regression will build:

$$Average = w_0 + w_1 \times A + w_2 \times B + w_3 \times C + w_4 \times D$$

Equation 8.5

Note that in this dataset, the label is the average of the four features. So the relationship is still linear.

A	B	C	D	AVERAGE
87	382	894	525	472
475	301	280	965	505.25
198	508	963	9	419.5
844	765	566	801	744
279	325	940	783	581.75
186	734	890	806	654

Figure 8.9 An example dataset with four features

Context

Exercise: Guess the model parameters

A linear regression model is training on the data provided in Figure 8.9. The Equation of the linear regression model is given by Equation 8.5.

What would be the perfect values for w_0, w_1, w_2, w_3 and w_4 that would capture the relationship between the features and the label perfectly?

Hint: The true relationship between the features and the label is given by Average = (A + B + C + D)/4. The label in this dataset happens to be the average of the four features.

Evaluate a Linear Regression Model

Linear Regression algorithm predicts a numerical value and hence is only used to solve regression problems. The metrics for evaluating a linear regression model are the same as the metrics used for any regression type of algorithm. Both Mean Absolute Error (MAE) and Root Mean Square Error (RMSE) are used to quantify the performance of the algorithm.

Given an RMSE value, would it be possible to decide if the AI is good enough? This depends on what is being predicted and how much error is considered acceptable for an application.

If you are predicting the price of a house and are off by $10, that is an acceptable value. However, if the AI is predicting the temperature and is off by 10 degrees centigrade, it is not an acceptable error. The scale of the label being predicted by the AI determines whether a given RMSE or MAE value is acceptable or not. For example, the scale of the variable being predicted in Figure 8.9 is (419.5, 744). This is essentially the minimum and the maximum value that we expect from the model. Errors should be evaluated relative to the values of the labels.

Pitfalls of Linear Regression

A linear regression algorithm can only predict data which follows a linear relationship like the one shown in Figure 8.9. If the data has a non-linear relationship like the one in Equation 8.6, linear regression cannot model it and hence will make bad predictions.

Feature	Label
2	4
1.5	2.25
3	9
4	16

$$Label = feature \times feature$$

Equation 8.6

Figure 8.10 Example of a dataset with a single feature and a non-linear relationship

Visually, for a single feature, examples of linear and non-linear relationships are shown in Figure 8.11.

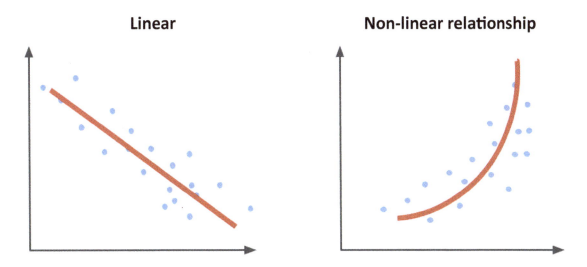

Figure 8.11 Example plots showing linear and non-linear relationships

This implies that linear regression is a good choice if the data inherently has a certain kind of relationship. In the real world, there are 100s or 1000s of features with millions of samples. It is hard to visualize or understand whether linear regression would be a good model for it or not. Therefore, data scientists often need to simply try it out and evaluate the results to find out if it is a good algorithm for the dataset or not.

Assessment

1. Linear Regression is a supervised machine learning algorithm (a) True (b) False

2. Name a few metrics to evaluate a linear regression model.

3. If a linear regression model has an RMSE value of 90 and another model has an RMSE value of 95.8, which one would you consider to be a better model?

4. If a training dataset has three features, `volume`, `weight` and `viscosity` and the label `density`, what would be the equation of linear regression for it. How many model parameters does it have?

5. Would an RMSE value of 100 be considered a good predictive performance for a linear regression model? Please explain.

6. Fill in the blanks

(a) Label value of a dataset used for linear regression should be of type _____.

(b) Within unsupervised methods, linear regression can only solve _____ type of problems.

(c) Unknown values of the linear regression model are called _____.

7. What types of relationship between the features and the label does a linear regression do a good job of modeling? Would it be possible to know by inspecting data, whether it would be a good candidate for a linear regression model?

8. What parts of a linear regression equation get populated after the training process is complete?

9. I have a dataset, where the label is `yes` or `no` based on three features, all of which are numerical. Can a linear regression model be used here to make predictions? Please explain.

10. What are some drawbacks of a linear regression model?

Online Activities

1. Linear Regression on the Fly

In this activity, students will see how linear regression fits a model on the fly as it sees new data.

Please go to the link: https://aiclub.world/fit-lines

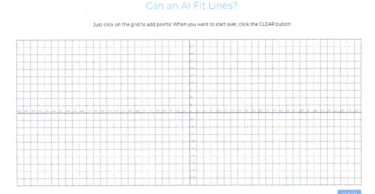

Activity:

Click on the 2D grid to add points and a line that fits the trend in data will appear as soon as you have at least two points. As you add points, the line will adjust to trends in data. You can clear the data at any time and start over.

2. Create a Linear Regression Model

In this activity, you can train a linear regression model on a large dataset. Please go to the link https://aiclub.world/linear-regression

One can use the pre-loaded datasets or bring in your own. Train a linear regression model and see how well it does. You can view the model parameters/coefficients and its performance metrics such as MAE and RMSE.

The advantage of this activity is that it caters to very large datasets.

Unplugged Activities

1. Visual Linear Regression

In this activity, students will draw a linear regression model and make predictions. They will also calculate the error of their linear regression model.

Activity:

Using Table 1, plot the points on a piece of paper. Let x-axis be the Feature and y-axis be the Label. Draw a line that you believe best fits the trend in data.

Feature	Label
4	7
6	8
1	5.5
5	7.5
9	9.5
2	6
12	11
7	8.5

Fill the table with predictions based on the line you have drawn.

Compare the predictions with the True values of the Label provided in the Table and calculate the RMSE and MAE values. This is the performance metric of the linear regression model created from visual inspection of this simple data.

Feature	Prediction	True Label
3		6.5
8		9
2		6
15		12.5
4		7

Python Exercises

Python code is provided in this module to help students get hands-on experience interacting with concepts covered in the chapter. The code snippets are kept simple and self-contained. All the code included in this book is available in a GitHub repository https://github.com/pyxeda/MiddleSchoolCurriculum/tree/master/Volume1.

A link containing the individual code snippets that can be opened in Google Colaboratory are also provided with each piece of code. When you go to the python notebook links provided with each code snippet, you should see an option to open in Colaboratory like the screenshot below.

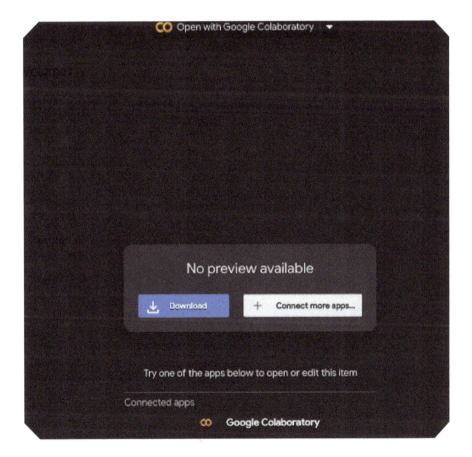

If you do not see this option, you might need to install the Google Colaboratory plugin in your browser.

Python Exercises

1. Linear Regression

What it does
- This code reads a csv file and creates a linear regression model (using scikit learn). Then, it evaluates its performance using MAE and RMSE metrics.

Link to the code in a python notebook: https://bit.ly/3LTdolR

Note that the above code can be opened in GoogleColaboratory. To view python code in this notebook, you will need the Google Colaboratory plugin installed in the browser.

CODE

```
[ ]  # Import pandas to read csv
     import pandas as pd

     # Import train_test_split to split data as test and train
     from sklearn.model_selection import train_test_split

     # Import LinearRegression class to get linear regression object
     from sklearn.linear_model import LinearRegression

     # Import metrics from sklearn
     from sklearn import metrics

     # Import gdown module to download files from the google drive
     import gdown

     # Import numpy
     import numpy as np
```

Python Exercises

```python
] # Please use the same dataset
url = 'https://drive.google.com/file/d/1Hxksp6KSjoex0wdER032QypLUYmdLNeg/view?usp=sharing'

# Derive the file id from the url
file_id = url.split('/')[-2]

# Derive the download url of the file
download_url = 'https://drive.google.com/uc?id=' + file_id

# Give the location you want to save it in your local machine
file_location = 'average.csv'

# Download the file from drive to your local machine
gdown.download(download_url, file_location, quiet=False)


] # Read the CSV
average_dataset = pd.read_csv(file_location)

# Get independent variable columns
X = average_dataset[['A', 'B', 'C', 'D']]

# Get dependent variable columns
y = average_dataset['AVERAGE']

# Split dataset into train and test
X_train, X_test, y_train, y_test = train_test_split(X, y, test_size=0.2, random_state=0)

# Use LinearRegression class provided by sklearn
regressor = LinearRegression()

# Train the model
regressor.fit(X_train, y_train)

# Predict using test values
y_pred = regressor.predict(X_test)

# Get actual values and predicted values into a table
predicted_results = pd.DataFrame({'Actual': y_test, 'Predicted': y_pred})
print(predicted_results)
```

```
[ ]   print('Mean Absolute Error:', metrics.mean_absolute_error(y_test, y_pred))
      print('Root Mean Squared Error:', np.sqrt(metrics.mean_squared_error(y_test, y_pred)))
```

Teachers Corner

Core Concepts

Linear Regression is the most popular type of regression algorithm in use today. While it is not suitable for every application, its simplicity and overall robustness makes it the first algorithm that is usually tried for regression problems. After studying this chapter, students should be able to:

- Understand what Linear Regression does
- Identify possible uses of Linear Regression
- Understand the limitations of Linear Regression and be able to identify cases where it is unlikely to work well
- Be able to measure the effectiveness of Linear Regression for a problem.

Grade Level Alignment

The concepts in this chapter are accessible to students in any Middle School or High School grade, with two exceptions.

- RMSE is challenging for 6th and 7th grade students and is recommended for students in 8th grade and above.
- Students who have studied basic algebra (in particular those who have learned equations such as y=mx+b) will have a greater appreciation for how Linear Regression can construct an equation to fit data.

The plugged exercises at the end of the chapter can also be used by students in any middle school or high school grade. The python coding exercises however, are more suitable for students in grades 8 and above, or any student that has familiarity with the following python elements

- Input/Output
- Loops and Conditionals
- Lists
- Modules
- Pandas and Dataframes
- SciKit Learn Module

The Curriculum section below contains introductions to all of these Python elements.

Teachers Corner

Tips

Encourage students to explore additional uses of Linear Regression with datasets that they gather themselves. What can they predict in their lives with Linear Regression? For example:

- Are their test scores proportional to the number of hours they study?
- Can they predict the prices of houses in their neighborhood?

Help students understand that for Linear Regression to work, the relationship between what is being predicted and the input needs to be linear. It does not require that when the input goes up, the predicted value should also go up. It is okay if the input goes up and the prediction goes down, as long as it does down linearly.

Explore cases where Linear Regression will not work. For example

- Can Linear Regression predict the multiple of two numbers. If there is one number A and a second number B, can Linear Regression predict AxB? It cannot. Why is that? It is because multiplication is not linear.

Curriculum

Full curriculum covering chapters 1-10 is available at https://aiclub.world/teachers-material-book-volume-1

Curriculum for Unit 3 (Chapters 7-10) is available at https://aiclub.world/teachers-material-introduction-to-ai-algorithms. Our teacher's curriculums include lesson guides, videos, presentation material, additional exercises, and assessments, as well as online support.

Scan the QR code for the Unit 3 curriculum (Chapters 7-10)

Scan the QR code for the teacher curriculum of this book

Linear Regression

Teachers Corner

Assessment Key

Answer key to the assessment questions in the book can be found here:
https://aiclub.world/teachers-material-introduction-to-ai-algorithms

CHAPTER

9

K-means Clustering

In this chapter, a popular unsupervised learning algorithm called K means clustering is introduced. This algorithm is quite popular and very easy to understand unlike other algorithms covered in this book. K-means clustering is an example of unsupervised learning, and can thus be used with data that does not have labels.

Introduction to Clustering

Clustering is an unsupervised machine learning technique that is used for dividing data into groups. Typically, these groups have something in common within themselves and some differences with data in other groups. For example, college students at a university can be clustered into different disciplines like computer science, economics, music, etc. Here, the common aspect within each group is that they are pursuing the same discipline of study. The primary feature based on which this clustering has happened is the *discipline*. This is of course an oversimplified example.

Real data will have more than one feature in it and grouping/clustering needs to be done by taking into account all the features in the data. There can be several different ways to group the data resulting in different clusters. Note that data does not have any labels in this case. Since the data does not need any labels and the goal is to simply group the data based on the features alone, it is an unsupervised method.

Figure 9.1 Example of a dataset with two features clustered into 3 groups

Clustering into different groups can be done in several different ways. For example, a data point may belong to more than one cluster. A college student may have a major and a minor in different disciplines. In this case, they can be assigned a probability to be in each of the clusters/disciplines rather than a single cluster/discipline. This type of clustering is called soft clustering. The other type, where the data point belongs only to a single cluster is called hard clustering.

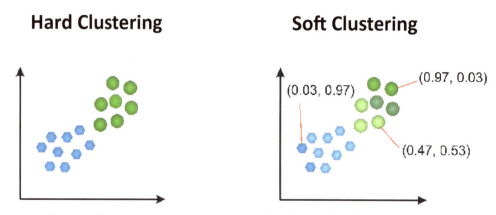

Figure 9.2 Hard and soft clustering examples, where the number of clusters is 2

K Mean Clustering

Types of Clustering Algorithms

Clustering data into different groups depends on the metric of similarity or closeness between different points. This leads to a rich array of techniques and algorithms that can be used for clustering data. In this module, a high level explanation of some of the popular clustering types is provided.

Hierarchical clustering assumes that data points in close proximity should belong to the same group. Measurement of close proximity depends on the metric chosen for similarity. Euclidean distance between points is a popular metric for measuring distance. One of the disadvantages of this method is that it is computationally expensive. As a result, it cannot handle big datasets.

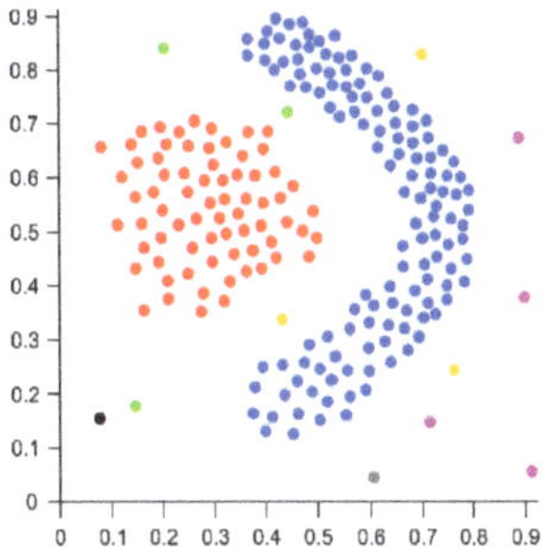

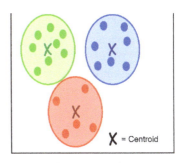

Figure 9.3 Clustering achieved by a hierarchical methodology

Centroid-based clustering groups data based on its closeness to the centroid. K-means clustering algorithm is a popular example in this category and we will explore it in detail in this chapter. The process of grouping data is done over iterations where the clusters get refined with each iteration till all data is stable and does not change its membership to groups.

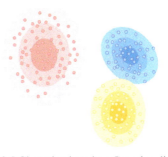

Figure 9.4 Clustering achieved by K-means clustering.

Distribution-based clustering methods group data based on the distribution statistics of the data. A popular example is the Expectation Maximization model. Data points that are more likely to belong to the same distribution where the distribution is of type Gaussian are grouped together.

Figure 9.5 Clustering based on Gaussian distribution.

Density-based clustering has a concept of noise or outliers in data. It groups data based on how dense the data is, where dense implies how close/similar it is. If there are data points that are relatively far from all other data points, they are not assigned a group and assumed to be noise.

Figure 9.6 Clustering based on density.

K-means Clustering

The goal of a K-means clustering algorithm is to find groups in data, where the number of groups is represented by the variable K. The algorithm follows an iterative process to group data and we will go over it in this section.

How does K-means find Clusters in Data

Figure 9.7 shows a plot of data, where there are only two features: weight and length. A K-means algorithm starts by picking K centroids at random locations. The value of K should be provided to K-means algorithm before it can begin. Depending on which random location the centroids initialize with, the final clusters can be different. This means that K-means algorithm can provide different clusters of the data points when run multiple times. Even when two different runs of K-means algorithm result in the same grouping, the name/number assigned to each group could be flipped. Figures 9.9 and 9.10 illustrate how the iterations in K-means progress to create clusters in data.

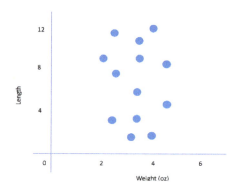

Figure 9.7 Plot of data with two features weight and length.

K-means algorithm in real life

Customer/market segmentation is an important application where businesses divide their customers into different groups before advertising or recommending products to them. In the telecom industry for example, there are a large number of customers with information about their usage patterns such as how they recharge, make calls, send SMS, etc. The analysis using K-means revealed 7 customer segments/clusters which lead to understanding the needs of each segment more effectively. This in turn helps the companies to cater to needs of different segments more effectively and retain their business with them.

Figure 9.8 Customer Segmentation

SOURCE - Bacila Mihai-Florin & Radulescu Adrian & Marar Liviu Ioan, 2012. "Prepaid Telecom Customers Segmentation Using The K-Mean Algorithm," Annals of Faculty of Economics, University of Oradea, Faculty of Economics, vol. 1(1), pages 1112-1118, July.

K Mean Clustering

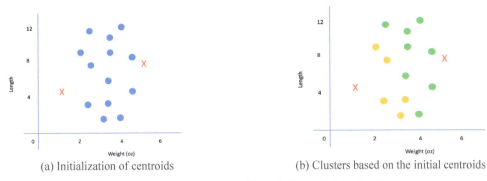

(a) Initialization of centroids   (b) Clusters based on the initial centroids

Figure 9.9: Initialization of centroids and clusters in iteration 1.

Figure 9.9 (a) shows random initialization of two centroids. After this, data points are assigned to the closest centroid. Figure 9.9 (b) shows the two clusters in yellow and green color. This is iteration 1 of the K-means algorithm. Based on the grouping of the points into two clusters, new centroid values are calculated. This new centroid location can be calculated as the average of the two features `weight` and `length` belonging to the respective centroids.

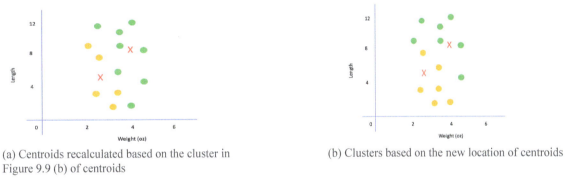

(a) Centroids recalculated based on the cluster in   (b) Clusters based on the new location of centroids
Figure 9.9 (b) of centroids

Figure 9.10: Adjustment of centroids in iteration 2.

Figure 9.10 (a) shows the new re-calculated centroids. Based on the new centroid locations, cluster assignment of the data points is recalculated and this is shown in Figure 9.10 (b). This iterative process is repeated either for a fixed number of iterations or till the data points stop changing their cluster assignment.

(a) Centroids recalculated based on cluster in Figure 9.10 (b) of   (b) Clusters based on new location of centroids
centroids

Figure 9.11: Adjustment of centroids in iteration 3.

Metrics for Clustering Quality

Clustering is performed in an unsupervised setting where there are no labels. When a clustering algorithm like K-means comes up with a grouping of data, how does one measure its quality? Metrics for measuring the quality of grouping are explored in this section.

Silhouette Score

Silhouette Score is a very popular metric to measure clustering quality. The score ranges from -1 to +1. A silhouette score of -1 is the worst possible value and +1 is the highest possible score indicating good clustering.

This score is calculated using two variables a and b. a is the mean distance between a sample and all other points in the same cluster and b is the mean distance between a sample and all other points in the next nearest cluster. For a single sample, the silhouette score is given by Equation 9.1.

$$s = b - \frac{a}{max(a, b)}$$

Equation 9.1

Mean value of the silhouette score for all samples is the aggregate score for an entire dataset.

Davies-Bouldin Index

Davies-Bouldin index is also a very popular metric to measure clustering quality. The score ranges from 0 to 1. A Davies-Bouldin index of value 1 is the worst possible value and 0 is the lowest possible value indicating good clustering.

This score is calculated using two variables n and σ. n is the number of clusters. σ_i is the mean distance of all data points belonging to cluster i from the centroid of the cluster denoted by c_i. The Davies-Bouldin score is given by Equation 9.2.

$$DB = \frac{1}{n} \sum_{i=1}^{n} max_{j \neq i} \left(\frac{\sigma_i + \sigma_j}{d(c_i, c_j)} \right)$$

Equation 9.2

How to Determine a Good K Value

The K-means algorithm relies on the fact that K is provided to the algorithm. However, in many practical scenarios, this value is not known prior to grouping of data. Two methods to figure out a good value of K are described in this section.

The Elbow Method

To determine a good value of K, one has to first run the K-means algorithm for several different values of K. Example in Figure 9.12 shows an experiment where the K value is varied between 1 and 9. The average distance of a data point from its cluster centroid is the y-axis. Note that this value is bound to keep going down as the number of clusters increases.

Note that the curve in Figure 9.12 looks like an elbow. As the number of clusters keep increasing, the gain one gets in terms of lower average distance from centroid keeps diminishing. Visually, one can inspect this plot and say that K=3 is the optimal value for this dataset.

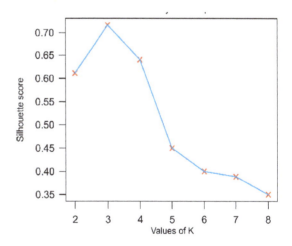

Figure 9.12: Illustration of the elbow method. The red circle indicates the optimal value of K.

Silhouette Analysis

The Silhouette score is a good measure of clustering quality. This score can be calculated for several different values of K and plotted with the value of K on x-axis and the score itself on y-axis as shown in Figure 9.13.

Since a high value of silhouette score indicates a good clustering quality, one can then choose the value of K that has the highest value.

Figure 9.13: Plot indicating Silhouette score for different values of K.

Note that both methods to determine a good K value need the K-means algorithm to be run several times with different values of K. This can be computationally expensive and is one of the disadvantages of the approach.

Assessment

1. Datasets used for K-means clustering have labels (a) True (b) False

2. What is the difference between soft clustering and hard clustering?

3. K-means algorithm does hard clustering (a) True (b) False.

4. Given a set of centroids that a K-means algorithm came up with, how would you know which cluster a given sample belongs to?

5. Calculate the centroid value of the following cluster, where the x-axis and y-axis value for each sample is provided in pairs [(4.5, 6), (9, 2.3), (10, 15), (4.8, 12.1), (5.1, 2.8), (5,12), (6,10)]

6. Fill in the blanks

(a) K-means is a type of _____ learning algorithm.

(b) K in the K-means algorithm signifies the number of _____ in the data.

(c) Silhouette Score is a very popular metric to measure _____.

7. Location of the initialization of centroids in the K-means algorithm impacts clustering quality (a) True (b) False. Please explain.

8. List some applications of clustering algorithms in the real world.

9. What are the different types of clustering approaches and which one of these approaches does the K-means algorithm fall under.

10. How can one determine the value of K to provide a K-means algorithm?

Online Activities

1. Interactive K-means Clustering

We will interactively look at how the K-means algorithm updates its clusters and centroids. Follow the QR code attached at the end or simply go to https://aiclub.world/clustering-visualization to start this activity!

In this activity, we will learn
• How K-means updates centroids
• How the data is divided into clusters
• How initial centroids impact the clustering quality

There is a video on the page that explains how to interact with the algorithm.

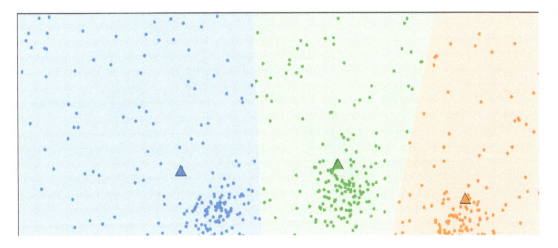

To do the interactive activity, you will need a computer with a chrome browser. Each time you start the activity, a different random set of points will be generated.

Unplugged Activities

1. Guess the centroid?

Guess the location of the centroid visually and compare it with the empirical value.

Activity:

Given the plot below, students will decide on a value of K and create K clusters. Each point in the plot has a corresponding index value to indicate the exact values of features on x-axis and y-axis. Once the clusters are decided, visually, guess the location of the centroid and mark it on the plot. After this, use the table below to calculate the exact centroid value.

Feature 1	Feature 2	Index
1.5	1.5	1
1.25	2.5	2
2.5	1	3
2.3	2.35	4
3.5	2.2	5
3.5	1.55	6
2.1	4.3	7
2.7	4.1	8
2.6	5.7	9
3.6	5	10
4.2	4.1	11
5	4.9	12
6	5.5	13
5.2	3.8	14

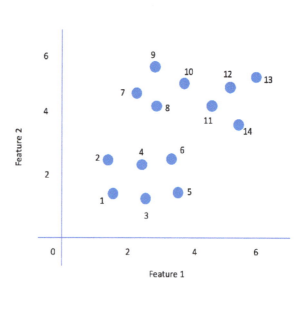

K Mean Clustering

Python Exercises

Python code is provided in this module to help students get hands-on experience interacting with concepts covered in the chapter. The code snippets are kept simple and self-contained. All the code included in this book is available in a GitHub repository https://github.com/pyxeda/MiddleSchoolCurriculum/tree/master/Volume1.

A link containing the individual code snippets that can be opened in Google Colaboratory are also provided with each piece of code. When you go to the python notebook links provided with each code snippet, you should see an option to open in Colaboratory like the screenshot below.

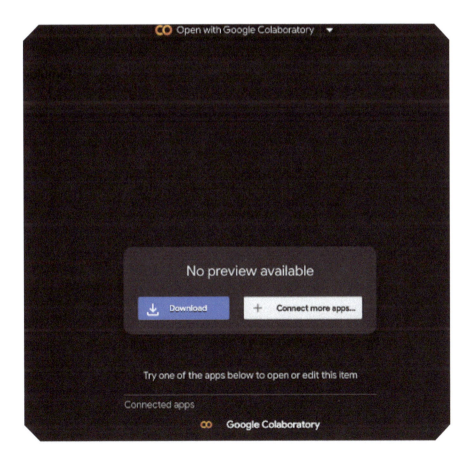

If you do not see this option, you might need to install the Google Colaboratory plugin in your browser.

Python Exercises

1. K-Mean Clustering

What it does

- This code generates random data in 2D and runs the K-means algorithm on the dataset using the value of k provided by the user.

Link to the code in a python notebook: https://bit.ly/3LPaVJ4

Note that the above code can be opened in GoogleColaboratory. To view python code in this notebook, you will need the Google Colaboratory plugin installed in the browser.

CODE

```python
[ ]  # Import pyplot to plot the graphs
     import matplotlib.pyplot as plt

     # Import make_blobs to generate two dimensional dataset
     from sklearn.datasets import make_blobs

     # Import kmeans module
     from sklearn.cluster import KMeans


[ ]  # Generate the two dimensional dataset
     X, y_true = make_blobs(n_samples=300, centers=4, cluster_std=0.8, random_state=0)

     # Plot the dataset figure
     plt.scatter(X[:, 0], X[:, 1], s=50)

     # Show the random dataset figure
     plt.show()
```

Python Exercises

```python
[ ]  # Mention the generated number of clusters and initialize the model
     kmeans = KMeans(n_clusters=4)

     # Train kmeans model
     kmeans.fit(X)

     # Predict the closest cluster
     y_kmeans = kmeans.predict(X)

     # Plot the clusters
     # Map each cluster to a different color using cmap
     plt.scatter(X[:, 0], X[:, 1], c=y_kmeans, s=50, cmap='viridis')

     # Get coordinates of cluster centers
     centers = kmeans.cluster_centers_

     # Plot the centers
     # Centroid color is black
     plt.scatter(centers[:, 0], centers[:, 1], c='black', s=200)

     # Show the clusters with their centroids
     plt.show()
```

Teachers Corner

Core Concepts

Clustering is the most popular use of unsupervised learning and K-means is a powerful and commonly used approach to clustering. After studying this chapter, students should be able to:
- Understand why clustering is a type of unsupervised learning
- Appreciate how clustering can be used in real-life situations
- Understand what K-means does and how it works
- Understand that clustering (and other unsupervised learning algorithms) cannot be measured in the same way that supervised learning algorithms are measured
- Be able to identify the common metrics for measuring clustering effectiveness and how they are used.

Grade Level Alignment

The overall concepts in this chapter are accessible to any grade level in middle school and high school. The silhouette score metric is accessible to any grade level, but may require additional effort to understand in grades 6 and 7. The other metrics (such as the Davies-Bouldin index) are better taught to students in 8th grade and above.

The plugged exercises at the end of the chapter can also be used by students in any middle school or high school grade. The python coding exercises however, are more suitable for students in grades 8 and above, or any student that has familiarity with the following python elements
- Input/Output
- Loops and Conditionals
- Lists
- Modules
- SciKit Learn Module

The Curriculum section below contains introductions to all of these Python elements.

Tips

Encourage students to find uses for clustering in their daily lives. For example
- If a child did not know the names Cat and Dog, would they still be able to group cats as one kind of animal (for example because they meow) and dogs as another kind of animal (because they bark)?

Teachers Corner

- How can clustering be used to find unusual events? For example - do thunderstorms behave differently from normal weather? If clustering were used to group weather events, would thunderstorms and rainy days be in different clusters?

Curriculum

Full curriculum covering chapters 1-10 is available at https://aiclub.world/teachers-material-book-volume-1
Curriculum for Unit 3 (Chapters 7-10) is available at https://aiclub.world/teachers-material-introduction-to-ai-algorithms. Our teacher's curriculums include lesson guides, videos, presentation material, additional exercises, and assessments, as well as online support.

Scan the QR code for the Unit 3 curriculum (Chapters 7-10)

Scan the QR code for the teacher curriculum for this book

Assessment Key

Answer key to the assessment questions in the book can be found here: https://aiclub.world/teachers-material-introduction-to-ai-algorithms

Deep Learning

Deep Learning is a large and important field of AI that uses a technology called Neural Networks. While neural networks have been around for many decades, they have recently come into prominence because they have been shown to be adept at creating AIs that can use rich data such as images, video, sound, text and so on. This chapter covers several types of neural networks that solve classification problems for images, and provides an overview of the field of Deep Learning, its applications, and trends.

What is a Neural Network?

Neuron

Before we can understand what a Neural Network is, let's explore a single Neuron. Figure 10.1 shows an example of a basic neuron, called a Perceptron. It takes in several values, applies some kind of mathematical function to them, and generates an output. Each input has a weight multiplied with it.

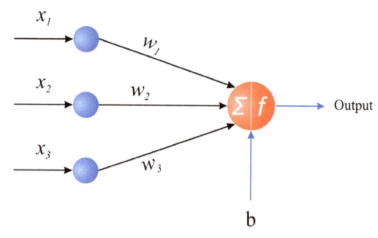

Figure 10.1 An example of a single neuron

By changing the weights, the neuron can decide to prioritize (or take more notice of) some inputs over others. It can even ignore some inputs entirely by setting their weights to zero. Figure 10.2 shows an example of what weights and a function can look like.

The process of training a neural network involves changing these weights and finding the best value for the weights. While this may seem simple for a single neuron, real-world neural networks have thousands of neurons and many millions or even billions of weights, making training challenging.

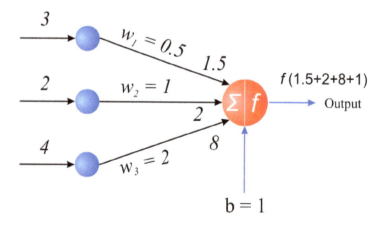

Figure 10.2 Example weights and function for a neuron

Deep Learning

A Neural Network

A neural network is, as expected, a network of neurons. Figure 10.3 shows a simple example of a neural network, called a Multi-Layer Perception (MLP). An MLP is also called a fully connected network. The network has an *Input Layer*, an *Output Layer*, and some number of *Hidden Layers* (in our example there is one hidden layer).

Each layer can have many neurons. In the example, the input layer has 3 neurons, the hidden layer has 4 neurons, and the output layer has 2 neurons. Each neuron takes inputs from the layer before it and sends its output to the next layer. In an MLP, each neuron is connected to every neuron in its neighboring layers.

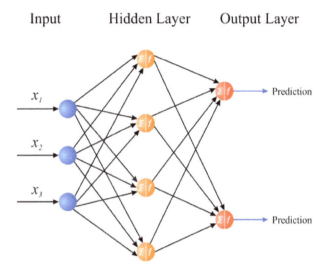

Figure 10.3 An example network of neurons

Context — Size of Real-world Neural Networks

The number of neurons in a neural network depends on its architecture. The number of hidden layers, the types of layers, the number of neurons in each layer, etc. all define a neural network's architecture and determine its size. In the real world, neural networks are used in varied applications such as image classification, language translation, question and answering, and more. A typical image classification neural network in the real world has 5,000 to 60,000 neurons. The architecture of neural networks differs between different applications, and each one is quite sophisticated in itself. The complexity of training a neural network is measured by the number of parameters rather than the number of neurons. The number of parameters is the number of weights in the network. Real-world neural networks can have millions or even billions of weights and can take hours to days (or sometimes even weeks) to train.

What is Deep Learning?

There are many types of neural networks, and they differ in various ways. Some ways that neural networks differ include the structure of the neurons themselves, the way neurons are connected, and of course the number of layers. This is where deep learning comes in. Neural networks with a very large number of layers are called *Deep Neural Networks*, and the technology to train and manage deep neural networks is called *Deep Learning*.

There is a popular *AI Challenge* in the images domain called *ImageNet*. Researchers all over the world compete and submit their models to it every year. The dataset consists of more than 14 million images. Deep neural networks have been winning this competition since 2010. Every year, the depth of the network that wins the challenge keeps increasing.

Figure 10.4 shows the history of neural networks over the past few years. You can see that the depth of these networks has increased substantially as researchers have discovered new ways to construct networks that can train in a stable and reliable way while having lots of layers. The larger the network, the more likely that it can tackle a tough problem with rich data like images and video.

Other factors have also helped researchers build deeper neural networks. Datasets are getting bigger. As seen in previous chapters, data can now be gathered from everything from sensors to cameras. Computers have also become more powerful. All of these factors have made it possible to create deeper and more effective neural networks.

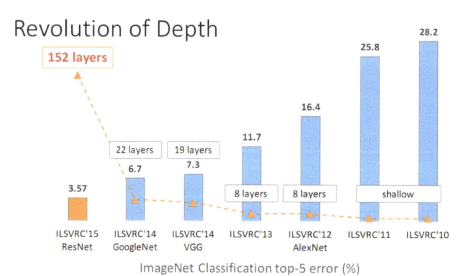

Figure 10.4 The depth of neural networks winning the ImageNet challenge, year by year.

Types of Deep Learning

As mentioned before, there are many types of neural networks. Similarly, there are many types of deep learning architectures that are used to train different types of neural networks. Some common types of deep learning are:

1. *Convolutional Neural Networks* (CNNs): These are popular for processing and classifying images.

2. *Recurrent Neural Networks* (RNNs): These neural networks are good for data that has some type of sequence. An example is a sentence where the order of the words is important to the meaning. A particular type of RNN is a *Long Short-Term Memory network* (LSTM).

Researchers are always experimenting with new neural network architectures and finding the best ones that work. For example, a very recent type of neural network, called a *Transformer*, has been shown to be really good at language problems (like question and answer or summarizing text). This type of neural network can also make some really cool chatbots.

Deep Learning in Self-driving Cars

Self-driving cars use a lot of deep learning technology. A self-driving car has many cameras within it that are used to take pictures of the surrounding environment. Using the AIs, the car needs to determine what types of objects are around it, how fast and in what direction they are moving etc. It needs to be able to identify other cars, pedestrians, bicyclists, traffic signs, puddles on the road, fires, and anything else it should expect on the road.

The technology used to do this is called object detection and object recognition. The first step is to identify the many objects in a single image. The second step is to identify what each object is. This also needs to be done in real time and very fast. There is no benefit in identifying a pedestrian after the car has run into them!

To accomplish this feat, self-driving cars use deep learning AIs that have been trained on massive numbers of images, trying to capture everything that the car may encounter on the road. When the car is driving, it uses these models to determine the objects around it.

 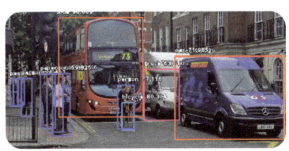

Figure 10.5 Self-driving cars and object detection

How Does a Neural Network Process Images

Deep learning gets its name because it is based on deep neural networks. Many of the deep learning techniques and uses are supervised learning. In the rest of this chapter, we will focus heavily on image classification with deep learning, which is a supervised learning problem.

However, deep learning is not limited to supervised learning. It can also be used for unsupervised learning problems.

Image Classification

A very common use of deep learning is for image classification. Figure 10.6 shows how this works. The concepts are identical to what was covered in Chapter 5 about classification. The only difference is that, instead of feeding the AI a table of data to learn from, we feed it a set of images. Since this is a supervised learning AI, each image is associated with its label (the right answer).

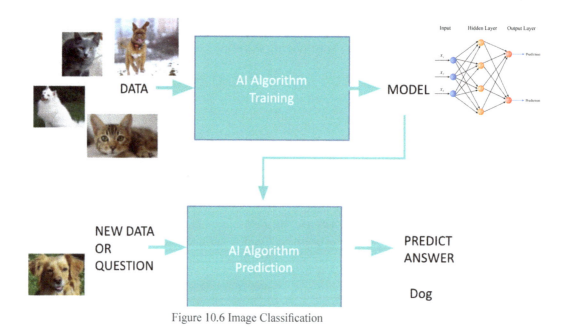

Figure 10.6 Image Classification

Accuracy and *Confusion Matrix* can still be used to measure a deep learning image classification AI. Training and prediction mean exactly what they did in chapter 5. The model in this case is the trained neural network with the values of all of its weights. The feature in this case is the image or a subset of it, depending on what type of deep learning is used. The dataset is the set of images, and the accuracy is still computed as before, using a random subset of the images as a test dataset.

Before we can learn how neural networks process images, we will need to learn how computers in general process images. Images are stored in computers as a set of pixels, where each pixel value reflects the intensity of color in a small part of the image. Figure 10.7 shows a pixelated image - an image with so few pixels that the human eye can see each pixel. While images like this can be found, for example, in very old video games, most images today contain millions of pixels and the human eye cannot see the pixels (this is also why the images are such high quality).

What is a Pixel?

In a black and white image - a pixel is a number that shows the grayness of that part of the image. In Figure 10.8, you can see that the white pixels are 1, the black ones are 0 and the grey ones are 0.5. Sometimes pixel values can also range from 0 to 255.

Have you ever seen a pixelated image?

Figure 10.7 A pixelated image

A color image has more information. Each pixel is actually three values, the *Redness*, *Greenness* and *Blueness* (RGB) of the pixel. These can again range from 0 to a max value like 255.

When a computer processes images, it sees the image as a grid of numbers if the image is black and white, and as three grids of numbers if the image is color.

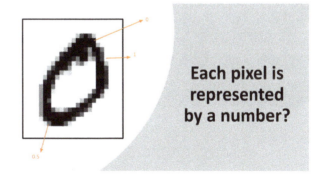

Each pixel is represented by a number?

Figure 10.8 Gray scale values of pixels in a black and white image

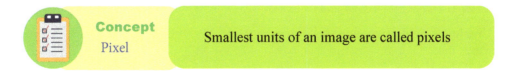

Concept
Pixel

Smallest units of an image are called pixels

Pixel counts in digital cameras over time

The metric most often used by camera manufacturers and marketers to tout their products have been pixel count. In the beginning, the 1990s—there was a great need for more pixels. But by 2000, pixel counts plateaued at 3.3 megapixels. At that number, the sensor was relatively cheap to produce, and the resulting images had just enough resolution to print images.

Nowadays, 12-, 14-, and 16-megapixel point-and-shoot digitals are the rule rather than the exception, and cellphones routinely offer 5-, 8-, and even 12-megapixel resolution.

What is a pixel and why should we care about how many we have in a camera? Essentially, at the heart of every digital camera is an image sensor. The lens focuses on photons reflected by the scene being photographed onto that image sensor. Etched into the image sensor's silicon are pixels (short for *picture elements*)—technically, photoreceptor or photodiode sites. Each pixel is a single point that collects the electrons, which are then interpreted into information about color and light. The signals from pixels are processed into a recognizable image. The more pixels, the more information collected and the larger the photo.

Figure 10.9 Images of cameras

REFERENCE SOURCE - https://spectrum.ieee.org/pixels-size-matters

Flattening Images

Now that we know how computers see images, how do AIs, and neural networks in particular, take images as input? For simple neural networks, like the MLP described earlier, this is done by a process called flattening. The grid of pixels is transformed into a column of pixels, and the first layer of the neural network will contain as many neurons as there are pixels. Figure 10.10 shows how this works. There is a 5x5 grid of pixels that has become a 25 column of pixels. The input layer of the MLP will have 25 neurons, each of which will read one of the pixels.

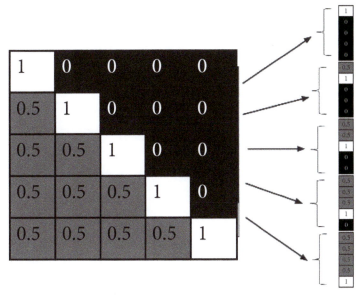

Figure 10.10 Flattening an image

Figure 10.11 shows what the image looks like after flattening. What this table shows is an example image with 25 pixels. You can see that it is a table, much like other datasets that we have seen before. This table can now be used by any AI algorithm to try to learn the patterns. Each image is a sample. Each pixel is a feature. The column name represents the row and column number.

1_1	1_2	1_3	1_4	1_5	2_1	2_2	2_3	2_4	2_5	3_1	3_2	3_3	3_4	3_5	4_1	4_2	4_3	4_4	4_5	5_1	5_2	5_3	5_4	5_5	Label
1	0	0	0	0	0.5	1	0	0	0	0.5	0.5	1	0	0	0.5	0.5	0.5	1	0	0.5	0.5	0.5	0.5	1	Diagonal

Figure 10.11 Flattening an image converts every pixel into a feature. Now the data is a table, but with a very large number of features!!

Figure 10.12 is another example of an image, with a resolution of 28x28 pixels. This is also a gray scale image. From the brightly colored pixels, it can be seen that the image is a handwritten 5. This image will translate into a dataset with 784 pixels. It is clear how the number of features can explode to be a large number when the number of pixels in an image is high. With images captured in today's cameras and phones, this is bound to be millions of pixels.

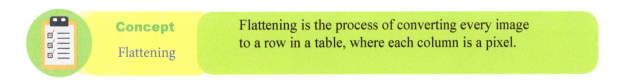

Concept

Flattening

Flattening is the process of converting every image to a row in a table, where each column is a pixel.

Figure 10.12 How a single black and white image of a handwritten number 5 converts into 784 features, one for every pixel value.

An MLP that can use an image shown in Figure 10.12 could like Figure 10.13. It contains an input layer with 784 neurons, two hidden layers with 16 nodes and an output layer with 10 nodes, one node for each number/category being predicted.

This is a very simple neural network by deep learning standards, but it is quite effective at detecting black and white handwritten digits. The sample images in these figures are taken from a famous dataset of black and white handwritten digits, called MNIST. MLP classifiers like the one shown in Figure 10.13 can generate accuracies of 90% or above for detecting handwritten digits.

MNIST Dataset

Context

The MNIST dataset is a world-famous simple dataset for neural networks. It consists of handwritten digits 0-9 in white on a black background. Datasets like this are great for getting started with deep learning.

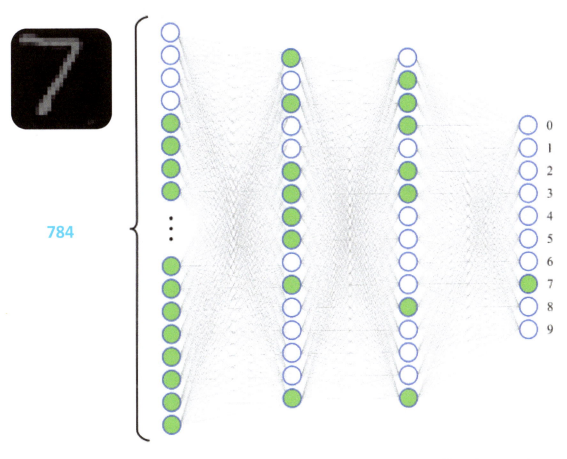

Figure 10.13 How an image as shown in Figure 10.10 can be flattened and input into an MLP, with 784 neurons in the input layer and each neuron taking one of the pixels.

Why not use Machine Learning on the Flattened Data?

Now that the data has been flattened and the collection of images are now a table, why do we need to use deep learning? Why wouldn't any other classification algorithm (like KNN) work?

In general, it is possible to feed the flattened image dataset into any machine learning algorithm. However, since flattening creates a very large number of features, the deep neural networks are often better at processing the flattened images. For a purely black and white dataset of 784 pixels per image, a KNN, as an example, may generate an adequate result. However, as the image size grows, deep neural networks outperform classic machine learning algorithms.

Inputs without Flattening

While simple neural networks, like MLP, take flattened images, their approach of creating one feature per pixel makes them impractical for modern color images which can have millions of pixels and three values per pixel (for RGB color). Fortunately, there are more powerful neural networks, like Convolutional Neural Networks, that can read images directly. They do this by a process called convolution, where they pass grids of the image through a filter (a simple analogy is a magnifying glass) and feed the pixels to the next layer. Figure 10.14 shows how a single convolution operation between an image and a convolution filter works. However, the output is shown for a single convolution. Convolution of the filter with the entire image is shown in figure 10.15. The complete convolution results in an output image of size 3x3 with a total of 9 individual convolution operations.

A convolution layer typically contains many such convolution filters. Each filter can be of a different size. The above filter was 3x3. However, there can be filters that are 7x7, 5x5, etc. as well. Each convolution filter can be thought of as a special type of neuron.

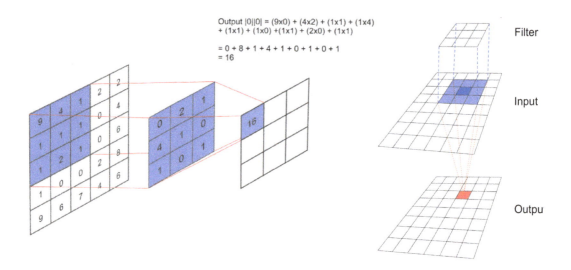

Figure 10.14 A single convolution operation with a 3x3 filter

Training a Convolutional Neural Network

When training a CNN, the images are fed directly into the first layer of the neural network (without flattening). The filters include weights that are set as part of the training process. As the training process occurs, the network "learns" how to tune its filters. In other words, the network decides for itself which aspects of the image will be the focus of each layer and each filter.

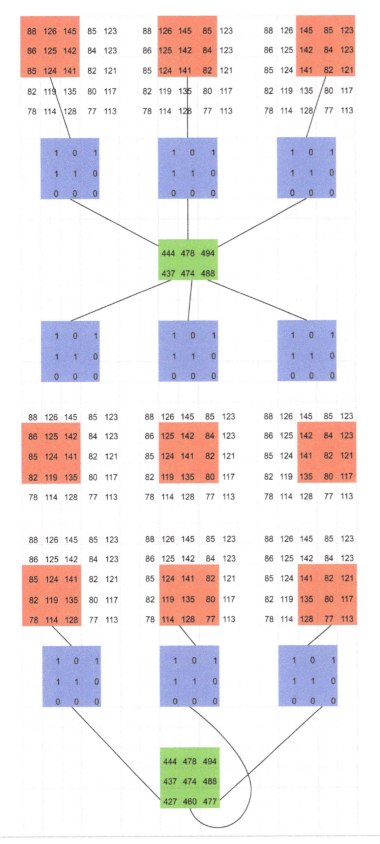

Local Receptive Field

Filter

Output image

Figure 10.15 Convolution operation on the whole image using a single filter

Can I assemble my own neural network? Or use an existing one?

It is certainly possible to assemble a unique neural network (and many researchers do this on a regular basis). However, for more common use, computer scientists tend to rely on neural network architectures already used by others. Why is this?

1. The neural network architecture is already proven for the task (for images, for example, the popular neural network architectures became so by doing well on the ImageNet challenge)

2. There are already software programs for them and it is easy to pick them up and train on your own data.

3. Training a neural network takes a lot of resources. Using an architecture that is already proven to work saves time.

At the time of this book's writing, popular CNNs that are often reused are the Residual Neural Network (ResNet), which comes in various flavors (ResNet101, ResNet152, etc.). Other popular patterns include MobileNetV2, Inception V3, etc.

Challenges in Deep Learning

Deep learning has achieved tremendous success over the last decade in many fields where rich data (images, voice, text, video, etc.) is used. Examples include self-driving cars, healthcare, agriculture, etc. However, the technology is not without its challenges. In chapter 4, some of the ethical challenges of AI included bias and environmental impact. These areas are more difficult in deep learning than in classical machine learning.

1. Deep learning algorithms, due to their complexity, are not yet explainable. This means that it is difficult for humans to determine how a deep learning AI made its decisions. If a deep learning AI is biased, or has learned bias, it is difficult to determine that the bias has been learned. Researchers are focusing on ways to understand how deep learning models work and new tools for explaining model predictions are being developed.

2. Deep learning models are some of the largest in the world. As an example, the simple linear regression models covered in Chapter 8 contained 10s of values in the model (the equation coefficients). The simplest deep learning models we covered in this chapter contain thousands of values in the model (the weights). This complexity is why deep learning can solve problems that conventional machine learning cannot. However, the size of the models makes the AIs expensive and resource hungry.

Trends in Deep Learning

Deep Learning is a rapidly evolving field, with many new inventions coming out every day. A few trends in deep learning include:

1. More and more data. Deep neural networks benefit from having a lot of data. Researchers are looking for ways to train with less data, but in general having more data helps.

2. Custom hardware. *Graphics Processing Units* (GPUs) are now used regularly for deep learning. However, new custom hardware is being built for deep learning because the AIs are so expensive and resource intensive to build. Google has built their own custom hardware (called the TPU - *Tensor Processing Unit*), and other companies are working on hardware architectures as well.

3. New algorithms and new networks. Every year new neural architectures are developed. Some attempt to solve harder problems or get better results on existing problems. Others attempt to solve existing problems nearly as well but with fewer resources.

Assessment

1. What is MLP and CNN short for?

2. What is the difference between a neural network and a deep neural network?

3. If the training images for a multi-layer perceptron have 20x20 pixels in them, how many neurons does the input layer of the neural network need?

4. In a 3 class classification problem, how many neurons does the output layer have?

5. Fill in the blanks

(a) A neural network is composed of a network of _____.

(b) A neural network is composed of the input layer, output layer and a _____ layer.

(c) Images are composed of tiny little elements called _____.

(d) The process of converting a 2D image into a 1D vector is called _____.

(e) A color image is composed of three channels, _____, _____ and _____.

6. A multilayer perceptron has 10 input neurons, a single hidden layer with 5 neurons and 2 neurons in the output layer. How many model weights does the neural network have in total? Please assume there are no bias values.

7. Explain the difference between a multi-layer perceptron and a convolutional neural network.

8. Neural networks can be used for both classification and regression types of problems (a) True (b) False

Online Activities

1. Image classification with neural networks

In this activity, we will understand how an AI can be used to see and recognize objects in front of it! Follow the QR code attached at the end or simply go to https://aiclub.world/image-classification to start this activity!

This activity has an interactive component where it will classify two different objects.

In this activity, we will learn
• Build an AI that can classify different objects
• Test the AI after building it

To do the interactive activity, you will need a computer with a chrome browser and a camera. You will need to have some objects ready, that you would like the AI to automatically classify. A popular activity for classification is mask, no-mask.

2. How do AIs see?

In this activity, we will understand how an AI can see and recognize different objects. Follow the QR code attached at the end or simply go to https://aiclub.world/computer-vision-activity to start this activity!

In this activity, we will learn
• How AIs can see using cameras
• How self-driving cars navigate roads
• How AI can play a game of recognizing what you draw

To do the interactive activity, you will need a computer with a chrome browser and a camera.

Scan for - https://aiclub.world/computer-vision-activity

Unplugged Activities

1. Create a Neural Network

Create a neural network manually to classify shapes

Activity:

Build a simple 2 layer MLP to classify the shapes found in the below figures. Note that this is a 2 class problem and the grid has a total of 9 independent elements. Think about how that translates into the number of neurons needed in the input and output layers of the network.

Squares

1	1	1
1	1	1
1	1	0

1	1	1
1	0	0
1	0	0

0	0	0
0	0	0
0	0	0

Rectangles

1	1	1
1	1	1
1	0	0

1	1	1
1	0	0
1	1	1

1	0	0
1	1	1
1	1	1

Report the accuracy of your neural network on the patterns below

0	0	1
1	1	1
1	1	1

1	1	1
1	0	1
1	1	1

1	0	0
1	0	0
1	1	1

Deep Learning

Python Exercises

Python code is provided in this module to help students get hands-on experience interacting with concepts covered in the chapter. The code snippets are kept simple and self-contained. All the code included in this book is available in a GitHub repository https://github.com/pyxeda/MiddleSchoolCurriculum/tree/master/Volume1.

A link containing the individual code snippets that can be opened in Google Colaboratory are also provided with each piece of code. When you go to the python notebook links provided with each code snippet, you should see an option to open in Colaboratory like the screenshot below.

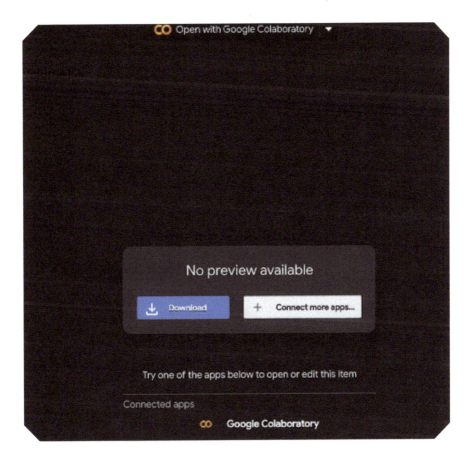

If you do not see this option, you might need to install the Google Colaboratory plugin in your browser.

Python Exercises

1. Convert a color image to gray scale

What it does
- This code reads an image, then converts it to grayscale and finally displays both images.

Link to the code in a python notebook: https://bit.ly/3v65DTv

Note that the above code can be opened in GoogleColaboratory. To view python code in this notebook, you will need the Google Colaboratory plugin installed in the browser.

CODE

```
[ ]   # Import opencv module to read, convert to grayscale and, to display images
      import cv2
      from google.colab.patches import cv2_imshow

      # Import gdown module to download files from google drive
      import gdown

[ ]   # Please change the url as needed (make sure you have the access to the file)
      url = "https://drive.google.com/file/d/1CokCuNkyP1zvuTXj_-hxIwevXz4TG9SA/view?usp=sharing"

      # Derive the file id from the url
      file_id = url.split('/')[-2]

      # Derive the download url of the file
      download_url = 'https://drive.google.com/uc?id=' + file_id

      # Give the file name you want to save it
      file_name = "dog.png"

      # Derive the file location
      file_location = "/content/" + file_name
```

Deep Learning

Python Exercises

```
[ ]  # Download the file from drive
     gdown.download(download_url, file_location, quiet=False)

     # Read the original image
     original_image = cv2.imread(file_location)

     # Output the original image
     cv2_imshow(original_image)


[ ]  # Convert the original image to grayscale
     gray_image = cv2.cvtColor(original_image, cv2.COLOR_BGR2GRAY)

     # Output the grayed out image
     cv2_imshow(gray_image)
```

Python Exercises

2. Resize an Image

What it does
- This code reads an image, then resizes the image to a fixed size and finally displays both images.

Link to the code in a python notebook: https://bit.ly/3LMBe2F

Note that the above code can be opened in GoogleColaboratory. To view python code in this notebook, you will need the Google Colaboratory plugin installed in the browser.

CODE

```python
[ ]  # Import opencv module to read, to resize and, to display images
     import cv2
     from google.colab.patches import cv2_imshow

     # Import gdown module to download files from google drive
     import gdown


[ ]  # Please change the url as needed (make sure you have the access to the file)
     url = "https://drive.google.com/file/d/1CokCuNkyP1zvuTXj_-hxIwevXz4TG9SA/view?usp=sharing"

     # Derive the file id from the url
     file_id = url.split('/')[-2]

     # Derive the download url of the file
     download_url = 'https://drive.google.com/uc?id=' + file_id

     # Give the file name you want to save it
     file_name = "dog.png"

     # Derive the file location
     file_location = "/content/" + file_name
```

Python Exercises

```
[ ] # Download the file from drive
    gdown.download(download_url, file_location, quiet=False)

    # Read the original image
    original_image = cv2.imread(file_location)

    # Output the original image
    cv2_imshow(original_image)


[ ] # Change the dimensions as you needed, to resize the image

    # Length to resize the image
    length = 224

    # Width to resize the image
    width = 224


[ ] # Resize the original image to the given size
    resized_image = cv2.resize(original_image, (length, width))

    # Output the resized image
    cv2_imshow(resized_image)
```

Python Exercises

3. Edge detection in images

What it does

- This code reads an image from Google Drive, then applies a Sobel filter to detect edges and finally displays both images.

Link to the code in a python notebook: https://bit.ly/3h2Ltlh

Note that the above code can be opened in GoogleColaboratory. To view python code in this notebook, you will need the Google Colaboratory plugin installed in the browser.

CODE

```
[ ]   # Import opencv module to read, filter, and display images
      import cv2
      from google.colab.patches import cv2_imshow

      # Import gdown module to download files from google drive
      import gdown


]     # Please change the url as needed (make sure you have the access to the file)
      url = "https://drive.google.com/file/d/1CokCuNkyP1zvuTXj_-hxIwevXz4TG9SA/view?usp=sharing"

      # Derive the file id from the url
      file_id = url.split('/')[-2]

      # Derive the download url of the file
      download_url = 'https://drive.google.com/uc?id=' + file_id

      # Give the file name you want to save it
      file_name = "dog.png"

      # Derive the file location
      file_location = "/content/" + file_name
```

Python Exercises

```
[ ]    # Download the file from drive
       gdown.download(download_url, file_location, quiet=False)

       # Read the original image
       original_image = cv2.imread(file_location)

       # Output the original image
       cv2_imshow(original_image)


[ ]    # Convert the original image to grayscale
       gray_image = cv2.cvtColor(original_image, cv2.COLOR_BGR2GRAY)

       # Apply the sobel filter to detect edges in given direction
       # If you want to detect edges only in horizontal direction, make dx=1 and dy=0
       # If you want to detect edges only in vertical direction, make dx=0 and dy=1
       # If you want to detect edges in both directions, make dx=1 and dy=1
       # You can change the kernal size (ksize) appropriately
       edge_filtered_image = cv2.Sobel(src=gray_image, ddepth=cv2.CV_64F, dx=0, dy=1, ksize=5)

       # Output the edge filtered image
       cv2_imshow(edge_filtered_image)
```

Teachers Corner

Core Concepts

This chapter introduces students to Deep Learning, an area of AI that has been around for quite some time but has grown tremendously in the last decade, showing capabilities not possible with conventional Machine Learning. All the algorithms covered in this book prior to this chapter have been Machine Learning. This is the first introduction to Deep Learning and the Neural Networks that make up Deep Learning algorithms. After completing this chapter, students should be able to:

- Describe different Machine Learning and Deep Learning algorithms
- Understand what makes up a Neural Network
- Be able to identify different types of Neural Networks and what differentiates them from each other.
- Describe the different layers in a Neural Network.
- Explain how Neural Networks work for Image Classification.

Grade Level Alignment

The concepts and exercises in this chapter are accessible for students in any middle school or high school grade.

The plugged exercises are accessible to any student in middle school or high school, who can use them to build an Image Classification AI with Deep Learning and explore how it works. The python coding exercises however, are more suitable for students in grades 8 and above, or any student that has familiarity with the following python elements
Input/Output
Loops and Conditionals
Lists
Modules

The Curriculums section below contains introductions to all of these Python elements.

Tips

Encourage students to explore what types of AI are suitable for different types of problems (now that they have explored multiple AI algorithms).

Teachers Corner

Encourage students to explore how images AIs can be used in real life, particularly in conjunction with cell phone cameras, drones, traffic cameras, satellites, or any other device that captures images. For example

- Cell phones today can sign a user in by recognizing their face. Is this a type of image classification?
- Can Image Classification be used to detect wildfires? Can it be used to predict the direction that a wildfire can go?
- Can Image Classification be used with satellite images? What kinds of uses are possible?
- Can image classification be used to detect rotten fruit? What other agricultural uses are possible?

Curriculum

Full curriculum covering chapters 1-10 is available at https://aiclub.world/teachers-material-book-volume-1

Curriculum for Unit 3 (Chapters 7-10) is available at https://aiclub.world/teachers-material-introduction-to-ai-algorithms. Our teacher's curriculums include lesson guides, videos, presentation material, additional exercises, and assessments, as well as online support.

Scan the QR code for the Unit 3 curriculum (Chapters 7-10)

Scan the QR code for the teacher curriculum for this book

Assessment Key

Answer key to the assessment questions in the book can be found here: https://aiclub.world/teachers-material-introduction-to-ai-algorithms

Dataset Resources

kaggle

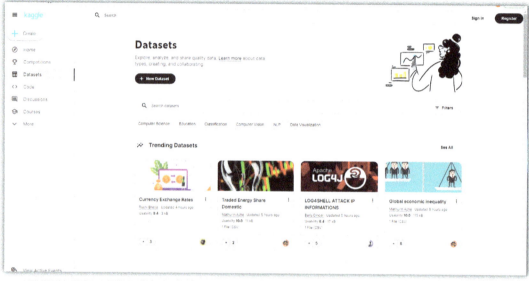

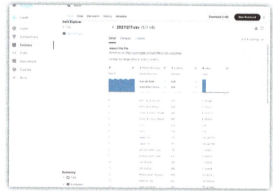

Follow the URL below or scan the QR code to access Kaggle!

https://www.kaggle.com/datasets

Deep Learning

Dataset Resources

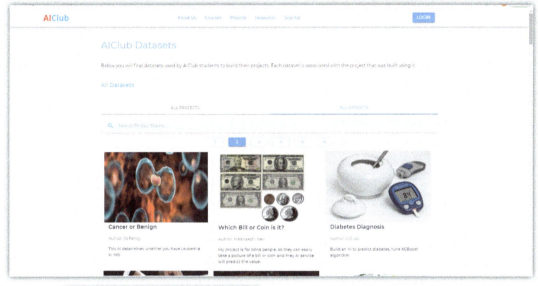

Follow the URL below or scan the QR code to access the AIClub dataset database!

https://aiclub.world/projects?tab=datasets

AIClub Student Projects

Build Your Own Projects!

Using the learnings from this book, you can now build amazing projects on any topic. Apply your creativity (the 4'th C) and build anything from simple projects that do not have any programming to building your own Python or Mobile Applications!

To inspire you, the following pages list projects in different areas. Follow the QR code to learn more and access resources including project videos and datasets to build the project. Some even have live AIs that can be tried from the project page.

Project Categories

1. **STEM AI Projects** - Use AI to solve a STEM problem, usually by detecting/ diagnosing a problem or forecasting the future.

2. **Social Good AI Projects** - Use AI to solve a social problem, usually by detecting a problem or providing assistance

3. **AI Powered Python Games** - Build a python program to play a game

4. **AI Powered Python Chatbots** - Build a python program that interacts with users and asks questions and gathers replies.

5. **Mobile Application** - Build an apps that interacts with users, asks questions, gathers replies, takes photos, etc.

6. **AI Recommender Systems** - Gather data from websites, data repositories (AIClub also has a large data repository for students use).

7. **Medical AI Projects** - Use AI to solve a medical problem, usually by detecting/ diagnosing a disease.

8. **Miscellaneous Projects** - Gather data, train an AI, use the AI to make predictions, use metrics to assess the quality of the AI, improve the AI by adding/tuning data, tuning algorithms or a combination.

AIClub Student Projects

Creativity

STEM AI Projects

STEM (Science, Technology, Engineering and Math) Projects help students understand how to solve hard problems with innovative ideas, state their hypotheses, gather evidence with experiments, and prove conclusions. AI can be used for STEM project such as detecting and diagnosing diseases, predicting the weather, helping address climate change, to improving diet and nutrition.

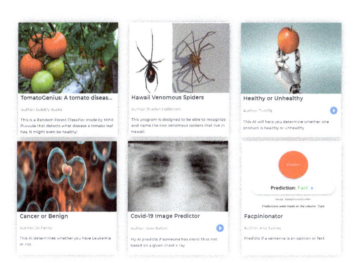

Scan this to find out more!

https://my.aiclub.world/stem-ai-projects

Social Good AI Projects

Social Good projects (projects that help people and communities) are a great way to develop leadership, innovation and entrepreneurial skills. AI can be used for Social Good projects from improving recycling, helping the blind, helping the elderly, providing medical access to rural areas, and more!

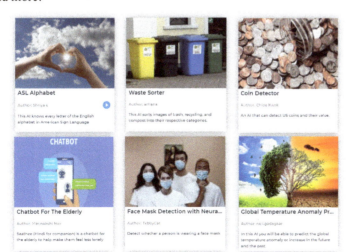

Scan this to find out more!

https://my.aiclub.world/social-good-ai-projects

AIClub Student Projects

Creativity

AI Powered Python Games

When Games and AI are combined, the AI can be trained to play to play a game, and then compete with a human or with other AIs! AI powered games can be used to develop coding skills, build powerful apps, and participate in entrepreneurial contests, coding competitions, hackathons and other challenges!

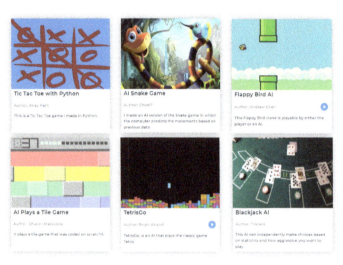

Scan this to find out more!

https://my.aiclub.world/ai-python-games

AI Powered Python Chatbots

Chatbots (software that talks to humans) are used by businesses all around the world to help customers, answer questions, recommend products and more. Building a chatbot develop important coding, application building and product skills that are useful in any industry. The sample chatbots shown here use AI to recommend products, food, games, answer health questions, and more.

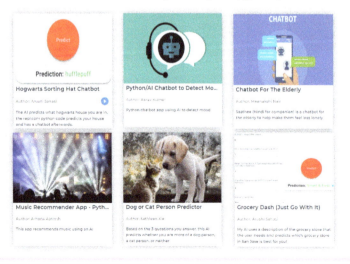

Scan this to find out more!

https://my.aiclub.world/ai-python-chatbots

AIClub Student Projects

Mobile Application

Building applications is a great way for to express ideas and solve real-world problems. App building also develops important skills such as how to build an application for a mobile device, how to connect such an application to an AI, and how to improve the app for their users. Examples include applications to assist the blind by identifying coins, help homeowners during natural disasters, play games, and more.

Scan this to find out more!

https://my.aiclub.world/ai-powered-ios-apps

AI Recommender Systems

Artificial Intelligence is used in many businesses to recommend products to their users. These projects harness AI to provide innovative services from recommending music and books to helping a user pick a great pet! Recommender systems projects are also great for entrepreneurial ventures, hackathons and other competitions.

TV Show Recommendations

Author: Sophie Yung

An AI that will use your age, recently watched shows, and preferred genres to recommend you a genre to watch.

AI Profession Recommendation

Author: Anouskaa V

The AI will predict what profession will suit you best based on questions you answer.

What's Your Movie?

Author: Bobby Jones

Predicts what would be you FAVORITE genre of Movie

Sport Predictions

Author: Jayen C

Predicts a sport from the given responses.

book_reco_feb2

Author: Dv Kalkin

predicting a book

Which Personality Type Are You?

Author: Preru B

Find out which personality type you are (out of 16 basic types).

Scan this to find out more!

https://my.aiclub.world/ai-recommender-

AIClub Student Projects

Medical AI Projects

Artificial Intelligence can be used for a wide range of medical applications, from diagnosing diabetic retinopathy, detecting risk for heart disease or diabetes, detecting fractures, and more. The projects provide an opportunity to analyze real-world medical data, train an Artificial Intelligence from the data, and measure and improve the quality of their solution. AI powered Medical Solutions can be submitted to STEM competitions, Science Fairs and more.

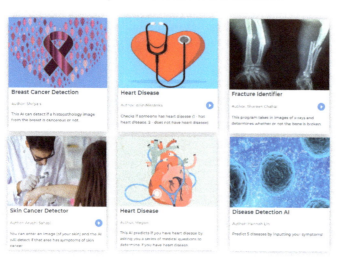

Scan this to find out more!

https://my.aiclub.world/
medical-ai-projects

Miscellaneous Projects

There is no limit to the ways that AI can be used! A collection of unusual and innovative projects are listed here.

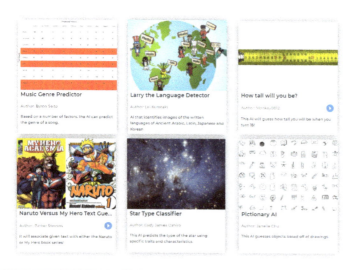

Scan this to find out more!

https://my.aiclub.world/
miscellaneous-ai-projects

Deep Learning

Reference List

Chapter 1

Figure 1.20 https://www.kaggle.com/danofer/compass

Figures 1.23 https://news.artnet.com/art-world/imagenet-roulette-trevor-paglen-kate-crawford-1658305
https://www.theartnewspaper.com/2019/09/23/leading-online-database-to-remove-600000-images-afterart-
project-reveals-its-racist-bias

Chapter 2

Figure 2.13
https://seedscientific.com/how-much-data-is-created-every-day/#:~:text=Every%20day%2C%20we%20create%20roughly,petabytes%20of%20data%20every%20day.

Chapter 3

Python Exercise Google Drive Link (1. Read Tabular Data)
https://drive.google.com/file/d/1sQGqysf7H
FPngnKgumOlzSmyI0CHgGkF/view?usp=sharing

Python Exercise Google Drive Link (2. Read Text Data)
https://drive.google.com/file/d/1HdBNGe8F
gwAeHUpMvlshzxxDi7OXqyze/view?usp=sharing

Python Exercise Google Drive Link (3. Read Audio Data)
https://drive.google.com/file/d/1QyDvZCcUmimEOw-
f1JIwohKvZoeAdRN/view?usp=sharing

Python Exercise Google Drive Link (4. Read Image Data)
https://drive.google.com/file/d/1kxJTOsYIWJ
GDpJ6MzrsIiy5RRynbTF6I/view?usp=sharing

Python Exercise Google Drive Link (5. Data Visualization)
https://drive.google.com/file/
d/1rL0yrArjx4fnXJrh8G1O6LemXT-8atsM/view?usp=sharing

Figure 4.9

Reference List

Chapter 4

Figure 4.13 https://www.facinghistory.org/resource-library/image/peaceful-protest-ferguson

Figure 4.6
https://becominghuman.ai/its-magic-i-owe-you-no-explanation-explainableai-43e798273a08

Figure 4.8
https://www.telegraph.co.uk/technology/2016/03/25/we-must-teach-ai-machines-to-play-nice-and-police-themselves/
https://en.wikipedia.org/wiki/Tay_(bot)

Figure 4.9
https://www.aclu.org/news/privacy-technology/the-computer-got-it-wrong-why-were-taking-the-detroitpolice-
to-court-over-a-faulty-face-recognition-match/

Figure 4.10
https://searchenterpriseai.techtarget.com/feature/FTC-pursues-AI-regulation-bans-biased-algorithms

Figure 4.12
https://medcitynews.com/2021/07/synthetic-data-a-new-solution-solving-historic-healthcare-privacy-challenges/

Figure 4.13
https://apollo.auto/synthetic.html

Figure 4.14
https://thispersondoesnotexist.com/

Pg 129
https://www.kaggle.com/c/deepfake-detection-challenge

Figure 4.16
https://arxiv.org/pdf/1906.02243.pdf

Reference List

Figure 4.18
https://arxiv.org/pdf/1801.04381.pdf

Chapter 5

Python Exercise Google Drive Link (1. Accuracy with Binary Classification)
https://drive.google.com/file/d/1Xi8i6GvjHS
OFb5X9G48aRUZFlHlF6zhI/view?usp=sharing
Python Exercise Google Drive Link (2. Root Mean Square Error)
https://drive.google.com/file/d/1jqwn3L8fV
Ex75W3LTojLXurjlOSz73BV/view?usp=sharing

Chapter 7

Python Exercise Google Drive Link (1. K-Nearest Neighbors Classification)
https://drive.google.com/file/
d/1vInPEsbpGgR89eLRIBNREIi-NN_Mo0KU/view?usp=sharing

Python Exercise Google Drive Link (2. K-Nearest Neighbors Regression)
https://drive.google.com/file/
d/1vInPEsbpGgR89eLRIBNREIi-NN_Mo0KU/view?usp=sharing

Chapter 8

Python Exercise Google Drive Link (1. Linear Regression)
https://drive.google.com/file/d/12gCImY1tXTJbii9p4Ubac35Cj7P-mpVi/
view?usp=sharing

Chapter 9

Python Exercise Google Drive Link (1. K-Mean Clustering)
https://drive.google.com/file/
d/10E3RIzNERwQH3TQ-jQaWqzbNCcmZArW6/view?usp=sharing

Reference List

Chapter 10

Figure 6.5
https://spectrum.ieee.org/pixels-size-matters

Python Exercise Google Drive Link (1. Convert a color image to gray scale)
https://drive.google.com/file/
d/1HPUyPqmAwJThSb_ZuyaEZEHlpsD0wjy7/view?usp=sharing

Python Exercise Google Drive Link (2. Resize an Image)
https://drive.google.com/file/d/1Q52PZCMj
pxLXL2JKrR8QgCl7FIgfGa4a/view?usp=sharing

Python Exercise Google Drive Link (3. Resize an Image)
https://drive.google.com/file/d/1-
Dyv9tEnbeApFi_wxs3Cw5yTzUOAPzSm/view?usp=sharing

Liked this textbook?

AIClub will be launching Volume 2 for 'Fundamentals of Artificial Intelligence' Here is a preview of what's to come!

Contents for Volume 2